Return of the Phoenix
Journey of the Master Key

A Novel by
Tania von Allmen

"Hold the Light High"

Copyright ©2011, 2012 Tania von Allmen

All rights reserved. No part of this book may be reproduced in any form, except brief excerpts for the purpose of review, without written permission of the publisher.

Sun Runner Publishing
Folsom, California
www.SunRunnerPublishing.com

Cover illustration, book design, interior illustrations
and typography by Tania von Allmen.
Photo for back cover by Caryn Joy, More Than Words Photography

Phoenix icon and headlines set in Aviano Serif typeface and glyph set.

Library of Congress Cataloging-Publications Data
von Allmen, Tania
Return of the Phoenix: Journey of the Master Key - Fiction. Raven Tahara is a modern mystic who intuits a new sacred symbol. In her quest to fulfill an ancient Egyptian prophecy, she must first transform every aspect of herself.

ISBN-10:0615548598
ISBN-13:978-0615548593
1. Mind, Body, and Spirit 2. Mysticism

Printed by Amazon Create Space for Sun Runner Publishing
in the United States of America
Second Printing: May, 2012 with updated Master Key graphic

Table of Contents

Prologue: *The Stone of Destiny* — 1

Section One: An Unlikely Destiny — 3
Scene One: *The Task* — 5
Scene Two: *City of Trees* — 9
Scene Three: *Old Soul* — 15
Scene Four: *Raven's Haven* — 21
Scene Five: *Layers* — 25
Scene Six: *Light Body* — 29
Scene Seven: *Seven Year Itch* — 35
Scene Eight: *Regression* — 39
Scene Nine: *Bennu* — 47
Scene Ten: *Galactic Underworld* — 51
Scene Eleven: *Energetic Wisdom* — 57
Scene Twelve: *Soul Prints* — 63

Section Two: Down to Earth — 69
Scene Thirteen: *The Bug* — 71
Scene Fourteen: *Good Morning, Sunshine* — 75
Scene Fifteen: *Vernal Falls* — 77
Scene Sixteen: *The First Gift* — 83
Scene Seventeen: *Temptation* — 89
Scene Eighteen: *Cathedral Rock* — 93
Scene Nineteen: *Dancing in the Street* — 99
Scene Twenty: *The General* — 103

Section Three: Bringing It Home — 109
Scene Twenty-One: *The Best Defense* — 111
Scene Twenty-Two: *A Good Offense* — 117
Scene Twenty-Three: *Judgment Day* — 123
Scene Twenty-Four: *Order in the Court* — 129
Scene Twenty-Five: *Just Following Orders* — 137
Scene Twenty-Six: *Facing the Fear* — 143
Scene Twenty-Seven: *Into the Fire* — 149

Section Four: Onward and Outward — 155
Scene Twenty-Eight: *Sanctuary of Grandmothers* — 157
Scene Twenty-Nine: *GPS: Guidance, Pre-Shasta* — 163
Scene Thirty: *The Road to Shasta* — 167
Scene Thirty-One: *Chasing Waterfalls* — 171
Scene Thirty-Two: *Return of the Phoenix* — 175
Scene Thirty-Three: *Connections* — 181
Scene Thirty-Four: *Seeds on the Wind* — 191
Scene Thirty-Five: *The Path Forward* — 193

Letter from the Author — 195
Acknowledgements — 197
The Master Key — 199
Resources — 201

To Max
*Who, in his quest to change the world,
started with his mother.*

PROLOGUE

FEBRUARY 14, 2011

THE STONE OF DESTINY

No human was present for the return of the Phoenix. Had anyone been awake before dawn and sitting in the park just outside modern Cairo, they would have noticed a solitary figure approaching a lone obelisk — all that remained of the ancient city of Heliopolis. Certainly they would have wondered where this woman had come from, as she seemed to materialize suddenly, as if through an inter-dimensional door.

The obelisk once stood proudly in The Temple of the Sun before the city was destroyed by the Persian invasion of 525 BC. In its day, Heliopolis was home to the luminaries of geometry, history, medicine, and philosophy. Plato, Pythagoras, Democritus and Homer were just a few who graced the courtyards of the most prominent center of learning in all antiquity.

The Egyptian priests of Heliopolis maintained its most sacred legend. Every 12,594 years the Phoenix would return from The Isle of Fire, the birthplace of the gods, and place a seed upon the powerful Stone of Destiny. They believed that when the Phoenix returned, it would usher in The New Golden Age — the Age of Aquarius. As centuries passed and piece by piece the temples and courtyards were destroyed or dismantled, the world forgot their story and no one stood waiting for the Phoenix to return. Today, no priests officiated the sacred rites, no fires burned, no songs were lifted up for this long awaited moment. Only the solitary obelisk kept watch... and waited.

This morning, cloaked in silence and obscurity, the Phoenix had indeed returned. Only an audience of angels looked on as this solitary priest of antiquity stepped forward and placed her delicate right hand upon the cold weathered stone. She closed her eyes, uttered an ancient prayer, and from her heart emerged a radiant sphere. The sphere of light appeared as a slowly rotating globe and wafted like a fragile butterfly on the desert wind. From within the sphere, jewel-like nodes containing every color in the spectrum of light sparkled. The glowing sphere moved out of her heart, through her right hand, and then permeated the stone of the obelisk.

The woman watched as light illuminated the obelisk and rose quickly like water filling a tall slender glass. Upon reaching the apex, the radiant sphere emerged and hovered for a moment upon the pyramid-shaped stone cap. It expanded to a hundred times its original size and encompassed the top third of the tower. The sphere was the Master Key that unlocked and activated the enormous power of the Stone of Destiny. Indeed, it looked like a giant seed placed upon the stone. As waves of light and sound radiated love, healing, and oneness from the Stone of Destiny, thousands of beings watching from beyond the third dimensional realm rejoiced.

Removing her hand from the stone, the woman looked up as the light of dawn swept across her face. She was given a vision of the light in the obelisk surging through an underground network and connecting the obelisk she had just blessed to other obelisks all over the world. As each tower was activated it too radiated love, healing, and oneness to its region of the world.

Looking up into the fresh new dawn, the woman searched the heavens with her mind and heart, *"What happens now?"* she wondered. It seemed she had lived ten lifetimes in the six months that brought her to this moment.

This is her story— the Journey of the Master Key.

SECTION ONE

An Unlikely Destiny

Scene One

Six months earlier...

The Task

Raven Tahara stared into the eye sockets of a miniature Mayan crystal skull. The artifact had just been introduced to her moments ago by Madame Zelda, a second story card reader that looked like she was one turban short of landing a gig in Atlantic City.

"And this," Zelda stroked the smooth crystal cranium, "is *Bernie*. Say hello to the nice ladies, Bernie," she said just before placing it back on a shelf behind her right shoulder.

Raven wasn't sure which name she found more unbelievable — Madame Zelda or *Bernie*. More unbelievable still were the circumstances that placed her here in this musty old Victorian.

Thirty minutes ago, Raven and Karly were en route to coffee when a young man on the sidewalk had offered them a leaflet for today's special on Psychic Readings. Raven suspected he was Zelda's son and working off his college tuition by proving P.T. Barnum correct. There really was a "sucker" born every minute.

Upon reading the leaflet, Karly squealed as though he were giving away puppies. "Oh my gawwwwd! I've always wanted to do this! I'm in. *I am so doing this!* I need to see if I'll ever have a love life." Before Raven could protest she found herself here, listening to Karly's "spiritual reading."

Madame Zelda hunched over a small round table and spread out a deck of tarot cards —inviting Karly to select five of them. The deep blue table cloth under the cards was embroidered with stars and crescent moons, and reminded Raven of Mickey's pointy hat in *The Sorcerer's Apprentice*.

Turning each one over in turn, Zelda launched into a detailed proclamation for every card. There were predictions for her health, her wealth, her career possibilities...Karly hung on each word as if Zelda were Rumplestiltskin spinning straw into gold.

Raven surveyed the cramped consultation parlor, looking for some kind of clue as to this woman's motive for impersonating a psychic.

On the shelves behind her were various titles on astrology, numerology, tarot, and a guide to crystals. Nothing stood out as alarming or unusual for the trade. Assorted stones and crystals lurked like mischievous gnomes between the books. Raven thought she recognized a cinnabar cluster, a beryl orb, and a cube of gold tiger's eye.

"Don't judge the stone." Raven reminded herself.

She viewed stones and crystals as "nature's hard drive" and believed that while each held unique properties, they could often be biased dramatically by how they were charged. Just as two computers could house identical hard drives with completely different content, one crystal could be healing while its twin could be toxic.

Like many relationships, crystals were influenced by the company they kept. The energy and intention of the person or environment that interacted with it could make a significant difference.

Following her gaze up the bookcase to the ceiling, Raven noticed a formation of four glass angels suspended by fishing line. They appeared to be on a direct flight path to greet Raven's new friend Bernie, his toothy crystalline grin gleaming over Zelda's shoulder.

Scene One: The Task

Zelda droned on for nearly twenty minutes, dropping in pieces of wisdom she apparently gleaned from *Fortune Cookie Monthly*.

Maybe it was the stuffy second floor air, the warm Indian summer light streaming through the painted shut window, or the hypnotic rhythm of Zelda's voice, but Raven was barely able to remain conscious.

"I am seeing a man in your future..." the psychic intoned.

Raven now understood why Bernie had no eyes. He had rolled them so many times they had fallen out. Raven was about to join him, when Madam Zelda turned unexpectedly and looked directly at her.

"And *you!*" A doughy manicured index finger shot out like a weasel from a cavernous sleeve. " *Listen.* You'd better get on with this "task" of yours or trust me... *it will be given to another!*"

Raven felt a weight on her chest that reminded her of a dentist's lead x-ray vest. Her lips stuck together. Her mouth had gone dry.

"How could she *know?*" Raven wondered to herself. "This *hack*? Wrong number. Wrong caller! *Right message.*" Raven had not shared anything about her life purpose or what she had discovered six months ago with anyone.

Bernie seemed to be laughing at her now.

Sometimes it seemed like everyone had a copy of the script for her life but Raven. She imagined herself to be the unwitting star of a reality TV show that only beings in other dimensions could see.

Raven swept a lock of her thick blue-black hair behind her ear, then folded her arms in front of her chest a bit defiantly. Karly snapped out of her trance. With the spotlight now clearly on Raven (wasn't it always?) Karly looked over to catch her response.

Raven, she thought, looked like a tragic heroine from a Japanese animé or graphic novel. Her black hair fell in a wing-like arc with the front longer than the back.

The window behind her cast dramatic shadows that highlighted both her fragile facial features and sculpted shoulders. She could almost see an artist's pencil sketching her into the frame.

Raven remembered to notice her body rather than the carnival sideshow around her. There was something about this place and Zelda's energy that made her feel like the lead x-ray vest had rolled into a ball the size of a grapefruit and deposited itself in the pit of her stomach. She also noted a sensation like an ice pick lodged in the right hemisphere of her brain.

Raven had learned to recognize and listen to what this meant. Alarmed, but informed, she decided she needed to get out before her friend Karly heard another word.

"We'd better go." Raven stood abruptly, cutting the session short as she shot a steely glance at Karly. Her look said, *"Why do I let you talk me into these things?"*

In a balanced, fluid movement enabled by years of tai chi practice, she nudged Karly's right shoulder with the back of her left hand, grabbed the dangling handbag from behind Karly's chair with her right hand, and arced it around Karly's left shoulder plopping it squarely in her lap. Raven managed all of this while taking three determined steps straight for the door.

Surprised and a bit embarrassed, Karly paid Madame Zelda and thanked her for her fascinating revelation about the man who would soon come into her life and how they were *so* meant to be.

As she spilled out on to the sidewalk, Raven brushed past "P.T. Jr.," who had sprung the trap just thirty minutes ago.

Scene Two

City of Trees

Raven was a solid three lengths ahead in the stretch before Karly reached the sidewalk. Raven wanted to blame Karly for her curiosity, but if she was honest, Raven would have to admit she would drop in on unsuspecting psychics to double-check her own intuitions.

While most of them were not in the same league as Madame Zelda, all of them spoke the same unnerving refrain, "You have a great purpose. You are running out of time. You need to get moving." And now essentially, *"If you don't use it, you'll lose it."*

"I thought it would be fun!" Karly interrupted Raven's reverie with her disarming perkiness. "Besides, aren't *you* into all this stuff? You could probably have given her a reading! I bet she would have liked that!"

"It's not the *same*, Karly!" she shot over her shoulder. "*Sheesh!* Didn't 'Bernie' give you some kind of clue?"

"Okay, so *that* was a little weird." Karly conceded. "But you have some crystals, and you have plenty of books like that."

Raven stopped and spun around, her eyes narrowing on Karly. "Listen. It's not about the *stuff*, okay? It's not magic and it's not a big game! Entertainment and information are actually different, you know, in spite of what we see on the evening news!"

Raven continued, "Karly, lots of people have access to other dimensional information, and trust me, some of the beings in those other dimensions enjoy having some fun with the *tourists!*"

Afflicted, Karly sulked. "Well, you sure did ruin it for *me*. I was getting some really good stuff. I didn't get my money's worth!"

"Don't be too sure." Raven walked on.

They each retreated to their silence for about a block, each pulling out her phone to check messages. Modern technology could be useful when you wanted to connect. It was also useful when you didn't.

"And don't even *think* of tweeting this!" Raven added. Karly stopped pecking her screen for a moment, then continued.

As Raven scrolled through her texts and e-mail, she recalled the days when she had sampled freely from the metaphysical buffet. Every psychic, card reader, lightworker, healer, numerologist, astrologer, or channeler had captured her attention. The more esoteric the better. Raven had been on a quest for truth and was certain the truth would be more interesting if sought in unconventional places.

She had learned, however, that discernment and discretion were crucial. This terrain was full of nuggets of real gold buried in wheel barrows full of manure. It looked like Karly had found her old license for driving the manure truck.

While Karly's reckless curiosity could be annoying, Raven appreciated that she was never a "downer" and always fun to be around. She was full of that "puppy energy" that could just as easily lick your chin as chew up your shoes.

The great cosmic comedy was that life had brought her another version of her former self in the person of Karly. Her interest in the metaphysical was very different than Raven's, however. For Karly, the unseen world was just another distraction (like dressed-up, lip-synching kittens on the internet)— just another wacky form of entertainment and amusement.

Karly liked to throw the "woo woo" lingo around and tell stories about her dabblings with other friends she perceived as not as spiritual. She had no intention, however, of digging in and doing

Scene Two: City of Trees

the messy work of personal transformation. She would rather live vicariously through Raven.

By the second block, they had reached a crosswalk and had to make eye contact again. Karly decided she would at least get the satisfaction of knowing why Raven was in such a hurry to get out of there.

"So... what do you think she meant by that bit about the task being given to another?" Karly waited a few beats as she watched Raven's face for signs of a break in her internal storm. *"What task?"*

"It's a long story," Raven dodged. "One I'm not really sure I want to go into right now..." Raven could just feel the Cirque de Soliel of thoughts whirling around on the tangled fabric trapeze that was Karly's mind. She suspected her response only encouraged Karly, who would certainly find the whole subject too irresistible to drop. Raven just knew that The Puppy had found a bone and the digging would be feverish and relentless.

To her surprise, Karly backed off. Instead, Karly was reflecting that this was one of things she loved about Raven — she was so interesting, so mysterious, and well, "cool". Karly also knew that Raven was very discerning about what she shared and with whom. You had to earn her trust, make her laugh (and most importantly) be patient. Raven wasn't about drawing a lot of attention to herself.

Raven's fascinating inner world and seemingly magical gifts were usually Karly's favorite topics of discussion. Karly fantasized about being able to do the things Raven could do. What frustrated her to no end was that Raven had not the least bit of interest in telling the rest of the world.

If Karly had even an ounce of Raven's gifts or potential, she would have hired an agent and had her own TV show by now.

She would proudly tell the world. She would use her gifts to really help people, to make a difference in the world. Oh, and live very comfortably. Don't forget that.

"How 'bout we get that coffee?" Raven suggested.

"Sure." Karly replied. "Isn't Old Soul just a couple of blocks from here?" As they walked along the tree-lined streets of midtown, the massive roots of the English elms, magnolias and sycamores lifted up intermittent bits of sidewalk.

On the blocks closer to Raven's redeveloped neighborhood on L Street, the sidewalks behaved themselves and featured crisp square nooks for younger trees. The arrival of mixed-use spaces with lofts above and restaurant and retail spaces down below seemed to be bringing more people back to the city. Sacramento had proclaimed itself the "City of Trees" for good reason. The canopy of leaves that arched above them over the streets was a diverse palette of early summer greens that shimmered as the sunlight peeked through when nudged by the gentle delta breeze.

Raven and Karly passed an eclectic series of Victorian era homes, artsy retail shops, inviting galleries, trendy apartments, and unique ethnic restaurants. Most of the city beyond "The Grid" (downtown) had sprawled into a dull monotony of predictable suburban housing developments, strip malls and fast food franchises. Mid-town, however, was an artist's reprieve.

Raven began to relax as she allowed herself to re-enter the present moment. Letting go of the recent drama, she found her breath and connected to the rhythm of her feet clicking along the cement sidewalk. Breathing in deeply, she smelled the earthy smell of old growth trees, and a certain mustiness of wood that permeates old neighborhoods.

"I remember when that used to be a muffin shop." Raven pointed to a dark green storefront with stained wood trim that now housed a seedy tattoo parlor. She noticed the second floor above the porch canopy was still the cheery yellow she remembered.

Raven was talking as much to herself as to Karly. "This woman I used to know ran a print shop around the corner. One day she chucked it all and started a muffin shop. It was pretty successful for a number of years. The ingredients were really fresh. All the muffins were made daily. There was original artwork on the walls—they rotated in new artists every couple of weeks.

"I remember driving all the way into town on Saturday mornings just to get a muffin and a coffee from Gail and hang out in a seat by the window and do some people watching..."

Karly sensed a shift in Raven's mood and remained attentive for the right opportunity to steer the conversation in a more esoteric direction. She had learned to wait for it.

"The thing I most loved about Gail's muffin shop was the sense of small town community." Raven continued. "People came in there week after week; they met their friends there. Gail knew all of them on a first name basis and greeted each person like family. There was so much love, you know?"

Karly nodded like she knew.

Raven continued, "This was way before there was a coffee place on every corner and the Second Saturday Artwalk turned every other building down here into an art gallery. Gail was an original. She was offering something thirty years ago that we now take for granted. She saw a great need in herself and in others, and she created a space for it."

"Did she make a lot of money? Did she sell the business, retire and go live the good life?" Karly asked.

Raven shrugged. "I don't know... My life got busy with other things and my routine changed. I stopped coming out this way. One day I was driving down this very street and noticed the muffin shop was empty.

"But what I always admired was the way she risked everything to live her dream, to run with her vision, to create what was in her heart.

"She created a space that nurtured thousands of people and she did something that gave us all a taste of something *we didn't even know at the time we needed or wanted*. We got a taste of caring and community. Yep. She was way ahead of her time..."

"Speaking of which..." Karly did her best Vanna White game show hostess impression, complete with sweeping arm and dramatic hand gesture. She swung open the door with a flourish as they entered the front door of Old Soul Coffee Co.

Scene Three

Old Soul

"Ironic." Raven thought to herself. Here she was at Old Soul with Karly. Karly was a decidedly "young soul" who really liked to think of herself as an "old soul. " Raven sometimes found it hard to believe that Karly was actually a bit older than she was.

Raven's observation was not one of judgement by any means, just an observation. She had experienced that some people had a sense about them—a "newness" while others carried themselves with a certain "knowing," a bearing that had nothing to do with their chronological years.

Raven was noticing more and more that many (not all) older people she knew seemed to have "young souls." They often saw the world on much simpler terms. Meanwhile, kids she knew like her nephew seemed to have "old souls". They frequently spoke with the wisdom of sages and could easily grasp very advanced concepts. (They were also excellent resources for trouble-shooting problems with technology. It was generally her nine-year-old nephew that taught everyone in the family how to program the DVR or use their computers.)

No matter, the aroma of fresh-ground, carefully crafted Artisan coffee was all she cared to think about at the moment. Raven ordered up a large Americano and Karly went for the small chai tea latte. As always, Josh, the young man in his twenties that took their order was a master of repartee and a genuine pleasure to encounter on their periodic visits.

Karly secretly wished they were "regulars" and could walk in the door and feel like the character Norm on the old TV show, *Cheers*. She imagined a room full of people shouting out, "Hey Karly! Hi Raven!" but she knew that stopping in briefly a couple of times a month would never get her there.

Old Soul was humming with activity on a typical weekend afternoon. The conversations of customers in the vast open-air brick warehouse building rattled around — simultaneously magnifying yet muffling them.

The old pane windows, painted cement floor, and distressed furniture gave it much of its rustic charm. The long brick wall to their right hosted a level row of paintings by a local artist; the hooks in the brick created fixed stages for an ever-changing cast.

Raven always felt her eyes drawn upward to the expansive ceiling with its exposed wood beams, shiny sheet-metal ducts, and skylights that punctuated what could easily have been a dark and utilitarian space. Instead, light poured in and illuminated the space and glimmered off the brushed copper service counter.

To the left of the entrance, wire shelving units on casters formed make-shift walls. The racks, weighted down with burlap bags full of coffee beans the size of cement sacks, formed a nook in one corner.

A large industrial grade grinder took center stage in the nook using the shelves for a backdrop and the sunlight streaming through the nearest window as its spotlight. Raven had the feeling they could hole up in the building for a month and never run out of joe.

Retrieving their order at the counter, Raven and Karly found a spot on one of the leather sofas and settled in with their steaming cups.

"So... how long have we known each other now, Raven?" Karly was going for the indirect, less-obvious path to the questions still simmering in her mind from twenty minutes ago.

"I don't know... maybe six or seven months?" Raven replied.

Scene Three: Old Soul

"In all that time, I don't think I've ever asked you..." Karly shifted her weight on the leather sofa, "about your heritage. You know, your background and stuff. You kind of have a different look about you that I can't quite pin down."

Raven wasn't sure where this was going but figured it was part of the price one paid to have authentic friendships. Besides, it really wasn't that big of a deal.

"Well," Raven replied, "I have a mixed heritage of sorts. My parents met and married just after college in Hawaii. My Dad was third generation Japanese-American and my Mom was Caucasian. Kind of unusual, since most pairings of those ethnicities tend to go the other way around.

"A few years after I was born, Dad got transferred for his job to the mainland and we ended up in Sacramento. I've pretty much been here ever since."

Karly could see it now—the rounder, more European eyes that were a striking blue-hazel combined with delicate Asian features and very thick, jet black hair. Raven was taller and had a slightly bigger bone structure than most Asian women she knew, but maintained a healthy athleticism. Karly couldn't help but think her friend had the perfect name.

"So 'Raven' is a pretty unusual name, don't you think? I've never met a real person named Raven before." Karly had her Barbara Walters interview groove in high gear now.

Raven decided not to comment on the "real person" aspect of the question and just go with her well-rehearsed story. She got this question a lot and had polished her riff into a pretty tight little anecdote.

"Well. There's an interesting story there." Raven took another sip of her coffee and settled back into the leather couch, crossing her legs at the ankles up on the wooden coffee table and holding her coffee with both hands just above her lap.

"My mother was a little bit of a hippie, I guess. She had a good friend back in college, her roommate in fact, who was of Native American origin. She taught her a few things about animal totems and symbols.

"I remember Mom had this little book she would refer to whenever she saw something interesting going on with animals in the world around her — like a hummingbird suddenly showing up at the kitchen window or a hawk circling overhead when we walked along the river on the bike path.

"Anyway, she and her friend were sitting around talking one day in the quad on one of those cement benches around a big fountain. Like many young women in college, they were talking about guys and marriage and how many children they might like to have. Mom said something about not being sure if she wanted children or not, that it was such a huge responsibility and she wasn't sure what kind of parent she would be.

"Right then, this huge raven swoops down and lands right next to her on the cement bench where they were sitting. It let out this loud 'CAW!' It totally startled my mom — she spazzed out and literally fell backward into the fountain!"

Karly almost snorted coffee out her nose. "*No way!* That is hilarious!"

Raven continued, picking up her coffee and taking another sip.

"Yeah, that made quite an impression! Well, when her friend had finished laughing and helped her out of the fountain, she suggested that maybe it would be appropriate to name her first child Raven.

"Did you know..." Raven leaned forward a bit, pulling her feet off the coffee table and back down to the floor. "The raven represents 'magic'? It is thought to be the Messenger from the Void or Great Mystery. Ravens are also about healing."

"I can't imagine a more perfect name for you." Karly agreed, shaking her head in disbelief. "That was a great story."

"So, how about you?" Raven shifted gears to interviewer. "Karly isn't a very common name either. Where did *that* come from?"

Karly shifted her weight forward to the edge of the couch and sat up a little taller, delighted to have the spotlight. She could barely hide her delight that Raven had identified something about her as "uncommon."

"Well, before I was born my parents were considering names for a girl..." Karly started in. "My Dad really wanted to name me

Scene Three: Old Soul

Karen and my Mom thought that wasn't unique enough. She had always been a huge fan of the singer, Carly Simon. So, they met in the middle and named me 'Karly' with a 'K'. Dad got his 'Kar' from Karen and Mom got to name me something unique that reminded her of one of her favorite singers, so everyone was happy.

"There ya' go..." Karly did a snap of her fingers and a little hand bounce off the edge of the table to add a dramatic flair and visual punctuation mark to her story.

Raven smiled and nodded as her eyes connected with Karly's — giving Karly a moment to bask in this feeling of being fully seen and appreciated. Just a couple of heartbeats, a breath, then Raven shifted gears.

"Oh, shoot! And there *I go*, alright... totally lost track of time!" Raven glanced at her watch. "I have to get back to my place and get some stuff done." Raven realized as the words left her mouth that "get some stuff done" was a very vague and transparent (not to mention lame) exit line.

The last thing she wanted to tell Karly was that she needed to get back to her apartment for some alone time to sort out this psychic news flash. So far, she had managed to keep the discussion up on the surface, yet congenial.

Fully enchanted by Raven's tale and satisfied with her own, Karly completely forgot to ask any of the questions she had been stewing over. They picked up their bags and walked out the door onto the brick alleyway into the late afternoon sun.

"Well, I better get back and get ready for the week." Raven said as she gave Karly a parting hug. "I've got quite a bit on my plate right now."

Raven winced inside knowing that she was still not "selling it" very well, but she was getting too distracted to care. Raven crossed the parking lot and set out alone for her place on L Street. All she could think about was getting back to her apartment and "unpacking" all of this. Raven had plenty of questions of her own.

Scene Four

Raven's Haven

Crossing L Street, Raven approached the front steps of her apartment just two blocks from Old Soul. Raven delighted in her new place — a California "Live & Work" interpretation of a Chicago brownstone. Raven's small design office was downstairs with her living space situated conveniently upstairs.

In the last six months, she had "converted" to Minimalism — not so much a religion as a movement. Raven had never really embraced the modern American sport of consumerism. She was cynical of fashion and had no appetite for the care and feeding of stuff only to relinquish it to the landfill. Following several bloggers who advanced the concept to the level of a social cause, Raven was encouraged. She was free to live out her proclivity for monkish simplicity.

"No more buying things I don't need, from companies I don't trust, to impress people who don't care." she asserted to friends and family. "If it's not useful or beautiful, out it goes."

Forthright with her decision, she never evangelized. Raven sincerely believed in actions over words.

"If it looks appealing to people, they are welcome to join me." she had told Karly. Without trying, she had put quite a few folks she knew on the defensive.

Even with her determined idealism, Raven secretly doubted that one person's choices could really change the world.

Raven was considering taking the simplification thing even further. She was considering a "car-free" lifestyle. She planned to ultimately walk, ride her bike, take light rail, or ride share to most anything that mattered.

Her decision aligned with her idealism but ran counter to her history. Raven had often identified with George Bailey, desperate to escape small town Bedford Falls in the old Christmas special. She had spent much of her life in Sacramento longing to be "anywhere but here."

Growing up, no one had much good to say of her hometown. How many times had she heard, "Well, it's *close to lots of great places*. You can reach Lake Tahoe, San Francisco, the wine country, the beach...all in about ninety minutes!"?

To make it all the more poignant was the knowledge she had been born in Hawaii. Some would say she had been cast out of paradise to toil among the Philistines. Sacramento was home to the largest collection of state and local government workers in the world — some 90,000 people.

To its credit, *Time* magazine had recognized the city as the nation's most ethnically and racially integrated city in 2002. This was a factoid rarely cited by the "close to lots of great places" crowd. Of course, they were often the same people who could still be caught wearing "Governator" T-shirts.

Raven's relationship with Sacramento had always been like a promising arranged marriage — something she was initially resistant to but had learned to accept over time.

Frisking her pockets for the last known location of keys, Raven bounded up the stairs and let herself in. She noticed her breathing become deeper and slower as she crossed the threshold. The scents of lavender and rose oils massaged her nerves as indirect, natural light beckoned retreat.

"Raven's Haven" is what Karly liked to call it. The feeling of her space was peaceful, artistic, and nurturing. Every color, original work of art, or piece of furniture was a deliberate and significant

Scene Four: Raven's Haven

player in this symphony of calm.

Deliberate in its absence and the first thing to be noted by any man in her life was the television. Raven streamed an occasional "must see" movie on her computer, but that was as much media as she could stomach. She wasn't sure what she found most disconcerting — the sensational doomsday predictions, imminent alien invasions, or pharmaceutical commercials.

If mass media were to be believed, every man in North America was doomed one way or another. If the vampires, aliens, or natural disasters didn't get him, he would still be unable to reproduce without the intervention of Big Pharma. No wonder anti-depressants were prescribed like, well, anti-depressants.

Raven hung her messenger bag on a hook behind the front door and made her way past the bicycle saddled with panniers in the hallway. She went straight for the kitchen.

Lifting the Michael Graves kettle off the burner, she filled it halfway with water. Setting the kettle to boil, she rummaged through the kitchen cabinet above the stove in search of her favorite tea—Honey Licorice.

"And here comes my Jewel of the Nile!" Raven turned to see her bronze Egyptian Mau, Isis, entering with a prolonged stretch that turned into a graceful strut. In stop motion she might appear to be skating across the kitchen.

"Hey girl."

The look Isis gave Raven was classic feline. She expressed mild disinterest, yet pleasure in seeing that her staff had returned to refresh the buffet and see to the litter. Raven reached down to scratch Isis around the ears and under her chin.

An approving "puuurrrrrrrr" and a bout of "wiggle-tail" encouraged a brief belly scratch. Isis darted away, startled, as the kettle began to whistle.

"Crazy day, girlfriend." Raven spoke to the empty space where Isis had been. Raven pulled the kettle off the burner. She refilled the cat's dish with dry kibble, then pulled out a cup for her tea.

Setting the cup on the counter, she dropped in the tea bag. Raven filled her cup.

Scene Five

LAYERS

Raven locked on to the red leather recliner in the corner; her approach maintaining the focus of a reconnaissance craft returning from duty to the Mother Ship. She landed with a sigh and swung her legs onto its matching ottoman. The window behind her cast soft shadows from the nearby trees onto the studio wall.

Clearing some space for her cup on the end table, she nudged aside a thick, green, leather bound journal. The gilded gold pages dared her to pen something deep and profound. At first, it had been the repository for her pain, doubt, fear, and relentless quest for healing and wholeness. It fell out of use as she focused more on living her life in the present. She had grown tired of reflecting on the past or attempting to single-handedly create her future. Most lately, she repurposed it as more of a field scientist's notebook. Ever since she had learned of her task, the journal had become a vault for her inquiries and discoveries.

The steam from her cup ascended to flirt with the air. Following it with her eyes, Raven's gaze was directed to the contents of the short cherry wood bookcase across the room.

Beginning at the top, Raven scanned the assemblage that made up her incidental altar. On the left sat an amethyst geode, then a collection of rose quartz Platonic solids arranged around a small citrine obelisk. Near the middle was a white stained glass lotus sculpture designed to house a small votive candle. Several family photos in coordinated frames capped off the right corner.

As Raven's eyes glanced downward to the titles on the shelves, she noticed—almost for the first time—the story they told of her journey in the last twenty years.

"It's like geologic layers..." she thought to herself. "I never noticed it before."

There was the illustrated King James Bible her grandmother had given her at six. Like the child who once carried it, the book nestled against the fully grown version to its right — the dark blue leather New International Version with two inch thick pages of gilded silver.

Fifteen years ago, she discovered the Christian classics and mystics: Augustine, Teresa of Avila, and Saint Francis of Assisi to start. Saint John of the Cross had been the docent of choice for her own Dark Night of the Soul. Then came Thomas Merton's *Mystics and Zen Masters*. "Our real journey in life is interior." Merton had said. Raven raised her tea cup in salute to Brother Merton.

From Zen Masters she transitioned to *The Zen Teachings of Jesus*, and then took an abrupt left turn with *Autobiography of a Yogi*. She found pragmatism in Jack Kornfield's *After the Ecstasy, the Laundry*. Titles in the last several years shed light on Mayan Calendar prophesies, the evolution of consciousness, and the collected works of Rumi.

Rumi and his elephant petting blind men had opened the door to Neal Douglas-Klotz and a sufi perspective of The Original Prayer. Raven smiled as she recalled the two years she spent memorizing, chanting and studying each line of the The Lord's Prayer in the original Aramaic.

Tucked away in the bottom right corner were the only two books she had purchased in the last two years — *What Tom Sawyer Learned from Dying* and Chesbro's *The Order of Melchizedek*. She acquired both books after her ordination in the Order of Melchizedek, an ancient priesthood named for the High Priest and King of Salem,

Scene Five: Layers

Melchizedek. It was Melchizedek who first introduced the concept of monotheism in the days of Abraham, and he was recognized as a priest of great authority. This modern priesthood, which spoke to some deep part of Raven's heart, was a simple and profound heritage of the original one. Each priest was empowered and encouraged to teach love and assist with healing in whatever capacity they were gifted to do so.

It had never been Raven's intention to start a church or perform weddings, but she had always felt inexplicably drawn to this particular order. "Called" seemed an antiquated notion, but that was certainly the case for Raven.

Halfway through the bottom shelf, her intellectual expedition careened into an assortment of Gnostics, Kabbalists, and theoretical physicists who had discovered the Divine in the most unlikely of places—*All That Is*.

Each layer divulged her intellectual quest —title by title, phase by phase. Raven wondered how many hours, how many years had been spent reading, seeking, discovering, learning.

Recently, however, the reading had become as pointless as a trunk full of encyclopedias on a rafting expedition. She had abandoned the trail of knowledge for the uncharted territory of "knowing."

Scene Six

Light Body

Raven stood and crossed the room to the book case. Pulling a matchbox from a polished antique cigar box on the shelf, she lit the votive candle within the lotus flower. As the flame caught the wick, her face was illuminated with its soft yellow glow.

Isis was captivated by the flame as it danced and flickered as it grew. Raven saw the reflection of light within her kitty's green eyes, the flame centered in her dark, slowly contracting pupils. The faint scent of warm vanilla filled the air. Raven returned to her soft leather lounger.

Raven settled in and sipped her tea. She breathed more slowly as she inhaled the sweet subtle smell of licorice. The warm air traveled down deep to her belly, expanding her diaphragm like a vocalist about to sing. The ball of warm air paused and seemed to fluidly turn like a swimmer making a turn at the wall. Raven felt the warm air rise back up into her throat and release from her mouth with a sigh.

"Aaaaaggghhhhhh..."

Isis looked at her with ears poised, her head curiously cocked to one side. The candlelight was still reflecting from her dilating eyes. Raven continued to slowly sip and breathe until half her cup was spent.

Setting the cup back on the end table, she relaxed her hands into her lap. Closing her eyes, she followed her breath inward.

"I invite the Light..." she prayed. "Please guide me."

Raven was well-practiced in her meditations. If there were frequent flyer miles for the terrain she had covered internally, she would have earned several around the world tickets by now. Raven was fully aware of the irony that she had lived most of her external life within a hundred square miles. Internally, she was a Vagabonder of the universe.

With each breath, Raven traveled deeper and deeper into the nurturing embrace of serenity. She first invited the aspect of Light she recognized as The Father.

Father energy cascaded down through her crown chakra as a steady, vertical, white golden light — like a waterfall emanating vision and loving direction. Raven observed this Light as it traveled like a river through her body. It quickly passed through her head behind her eyes and nose, then seemed to flow around an area in her throat like a stream passing around a small boulder.

The Light continued to move easily through her heart, then encountered another obstacle in her stomach. Raven continued to breathe and observe the flow, noticing where it traveled smoothly and where it seemed to get stuck. She allowed the Light to flow completely through all the way out her feet.

As she reached the still point, Raven focused her attention on the areas where she experienced the Light not flowing. With her awareness, she felt into these places to see what would come up.

Like a movie beginning in a darkened theater, an image appeared in her mind's eye. Raven saw herself walking down the middle of a cobblestone street in a small village. Along her route she saw people who reminded her of the people she had dealt with earlier that day.

There was her friend, Karly, asking all kinds of questions. There was the psychic, looking like a gypsy fortune teller complete with shawl around her head and large hoop earrings. She kept yelling from her wagon, "If you don't do something with it, the task will be given to another!" Then the fortune teller would laugh with

Scene Six: Light Body

a cackle. She appeared to be getting voice coaching from the Wicked Witch of the East.

Raven walked on past various scenes and conversations, continuing straight out of town to a meadow full of tall green grass with wildflowers. She walked through a field of gnarly oaks, then a misty coastal cliff lined with redwood sentinels. As dusk gave way to nightfall, she reached the edge of the cliff where a precipice jutted out like a large stone finger into the darkness. Raven saw her self walk out to the edge, sit down, and look out into the Void. She sat there for some time, asking to see what she needed to see.

Out of the Void, a spotlight from an indeterminate source illuminated an oblong white shape in front of her. Like a chrysalis suspended from above, it was tapered on the top and bottom. Layer upon layer of thin web-like threads about the thickness of kite string created a gauzy texture.

Raven watched the shape slowly turn counterclockwise. As it turned, the white threads began to fall away and land below onto the ground near Raven's feet. The shape gradually spun faster and faster, with each turn shedding more and more layers of the silky white thread. As the layers fell away, Raven witnessed what looked like a radiant light beginning to shine through the threads, and glow with a beautiful softness.

When all the threads had nearly fallen away, what remained was a light being—a woman with Raven's proportions. In fact, Raven instantly knew in looking at her that she was witnessing some aspect of herself. The light being, now free from her bonds, began to twirl and spin—much like the steam in her cup moments ago.

She gracefully danced in air, her radiance illuminating the darkness around her. As she danced, the light being gestured outward, as if tossing a stone into some unseen pond.

Small rays of light flowed out from her hands with glowing balls of light traveling far off into the distance. Many hundreds of "light salvos" pierced the darkness and fixed themselves in position as stars in the night sky.

Gradually, the spaces between the lights became less and less and the strength of the light became greater and greater until finally the entire sky above Raven was as bright as the noonday sun. All the light became one, and the light being was one with that light.

Raven sat in wonder.

She brought her awareness back to her body and felt it filled with the peace and joy of this amazing vision. She felt inspired, encouraged, but mostly just completely loved. Deep down, she knew that this was the essence of her "task" and that somehow the symbol she had intuited had something to do with it.

The remaining questions were "what?" and "how?" She could not begin to imagine, "why?"

Raven emerged from the solace of her meditation and spent a few moments capturing it in her leather journal. Across the room she heard her cell phone, still in her bag, vibrate with a new voice message.

Raven got up and checked the phone. The voice mail cue read "Ania."

"Somehow she just always knows..." Raven thought, shaking her head. Seeing Ania's name in her message cue added the punctuation to her meditation. It was time to get some input from the one who had taught her to tell the gold from the manure.

Raven needed to rid herself of the self-doubt and second guessing. She needed to take another step forward.

Over the last seven years, Raven had witnessed numerous demonstrations of Ania's discernment of the subtleties of energetic vibrations. She was like a wine connoisseur of energy. Where Raven could now discern a "Bordeaux" from a "Piñot Noir", Ania could take a sip of the Bordeaux and tell you much more than the type of wine, the wine-maker, and the year. She could run down the vat number in which it matured, the location of the field, and the soil contents that gave it its unique fruity flavor.

Raven also imagined, with a chuckle, her friend would also sense what traumatic event had happened when the wine-maker was five. Perhaps the trauma of his father's rejection of him as a child would be discovered to be the pivotal event that led him to forsake the family dairy empire and become a wine maker.

The information Raven received six months ago about her

Scene Six: Light Body

task had inspired her to intuit and create a very significant and powerful symbol. Raven believed that it captured the essence of a new level of consciousness—one of love, healing, wholeness, and integrated balance. Still, Raven second-guessed her abilities.

It was time to double-check her "homework". If Raven had created a symbol based on something harmful or deceptive, it would never pass Ania's test. Only something that held the vibration of love—that was fully balanced—would get her approval.

Raven pulled out her laptop, searched for the folder marked "Master Key" and found a copy of the symbol. Attaching the image to the e-mail, Raven chose her words carefully.

She did her best to sound casual, in spite of the enormity of weight she had placed on the outcome.

Raven wrote,

Got your voicemail. Great to hear from you! Hey, just wanted you to have a look at this symbol I've been intuiting over the last few months. How does it feel to you?
Love,
Raven

Raven hit "Send. "She said a little prayer, "Please. Please. Don't let it be 'sweet and shiny'. If this thing is all jacked up... If I got it totally wrong... if I have been deceived into a big illusion to gratify my ego, let it end now. I won't take another step. I surrender the outcome."

She imagined the file shooting its way like a laser through the tangled web of cyberspace.

Raven reflected on the long strange journey that brought her to this moment. Most especially the fact that it was Ania who had discovered her unusual gift for being able to focus on a person or business and intuitively capture its "vibration" or core essence as a symbol. In Ania's "engineer speak," Raven was intuitively performing "Fourier transformations" — seamlessly converting waves to matter.

For the last several years, Raven had begun integrating this ability into her design work. Project by project, client by client, she honed her abilities until she was now doing it instantaneously.

She could just focus on a person or organization, ask to see the symbol for their core essence, and see it materialize fully in her mind's eye. Decades ago, she would spend hours thinking and sketching her way through dozens of haphazard experiments. Today she created spontaneously and immediately.

Sometimes, what came to mind intuitively was so unexpected, so captivating, so beautiful, that it not only impressed her clients, but startled Raven as well. Just last week, Raven had shown one of her designs to a client who had welled up with tears of emotion.

She gasped, "Oh my God... It's perfect. It's beautiful."

After a moment to recompose herself, the client smiled. "I can't think of a single thing I would change."

It was at the height of this full acceptance of her gifts and abilities that Raven learned about "the task."

The "ping" from Raven's computer snapped her back to the present moment. She clicked on her e-mail to see if it was a message from Ania. Raven took a deep breath...

Yes. There she was.

Raven held her breath again as she clicked open the message, then exhaled deeply as the words materialized on the screen. Months of self-doubt and second guessing fell from her shoulders like a Los Angeles mud slide with just two words, "Looks good."

As Raven stared at the screen in relief, she heard the sound of bells ringing at St. John's down the street. With each ring, she noticed the area in her throat becoming more agitated.

Another "ping" sounded on her laptop. This too was a message from Ania. "Come for session."

Scene Seven

Seven Year Itch

"Seven years." Raven thought as she cruised up Interstate 80 to Grass Valley. She had heard somewhere that the human body completely regenerates itself every seven years. This was also the number of years she had known Ania. Raven was convinced that every cell in her body had completely transformed in that time.

Raven had begun this journey seeking to ascend higher levels of consciousness through greater knowledge. She never imagined it would require her to plumb the depths of her soul. Each layer she peeled away exposed more and more of her heart, and at times she felt so vulnerable she was afraid to go further.

Like her meditation several days ago, she had unraveled her defenses and barriers to love until she was literally becoming that love. And Love, she believed, represented the highest possible level of consciousness.

This is what she had sought with such fervor for over twenty-five years. Still, the layers seemed endless.

Raven thought back to that first workshop seven years ago. Lost in the dark on the winding foothill roads on a cold December evening, she was about to give up and go home. Midway through her U-turn, her headlights caught the street sign she had been looking for. How would her life have been different had she given up and gone home that crisp December evening?

Raven wondered.

She imagined some unseen angel whispering in her ear that night to slow down. Turn here. Look there. Nothing had been the same since.

Pulling up the driveway, Raven remembered the first time she saw this house tucked away in the foothills. The warm glow of the houselights was set against the pitch dark hillside. It reminded Raven of a lantern adrift and floating on a pond. A wisp of smoke curled out the chimney from the pot belly stove waiting inside. A bearded man wearing a fleece jacket stepped out onto the porch and carried in a load of firewood.

She remembered the mixed feelings that wrestled within as she parked the car in the driveway that evening.

Excitement for the new.

Hope for the possibilities.

Nervous. She did not know why.

Back in the present, Raven walked up the porch steps as she had done hundreds of times before and knocked on the sturdy wooden door. Ania swung the door open and leaned slightly into the door frame. She was tall, slim, and her blue eyes exuded an inner light that made her driver's license appear to be a forgery.

"Allo." Ania smiled at her old friend.

Raven delighted in Ania's Polish accent. It had become endearing to her over the years. Raven giggled inwardly and smiled to herself thinking about the time she had mistaken her pronunciation of "sheet". Ania was "going to geev her sheet" and it sounded more like a warning than an offer of linens.

Even after several decades in the states, Ania still sounded a few degrees in latitude off Natasha the spy from the old Bullwinkle cartoons Raven had grown up with. This was the voice that had narrated Raven's many inward journeys.

Raven smiled back and offered a hug. Making an attempt at small talk, Raven offered, "Remember my friend, Karly? You would not believe what she got us into a few days ago!"

Scene Seven: Seven Year Itch

"The one you like to call your "Mini-Me?" The one who is always asking you so many questions?" Ania countered.

"Yes. That one." Raven replied.

"Ah, yes. I remember her now. I call her *Payback!*" Ania laughed impishly at her joke and clapped her hands together. She had earned it. Raven had been her Karly.

"What is going on with your throat?" Ania got to the point.

"I bumped into something that has me afraid to speak my truth." Raven offered, pleased she had gotten that far. "I think it has something to do with that symbol I sent you."

"Could be." Ania replied. "Let's have a look."

Scene Eight

Regression

Raven and Ania walked across the living room where Raven had spent untold hours learning to meditate. They walked across the hardwood floors past the windowed alcove typically furnished with two massage tables during workshop sessions.

Raven wondered how many buckets of tears she had shed on those tables. How many treasures had she gleaned from spelunking into the dark caverns of her psyche?

Seven years of practice had brought her to the place where she could get many of her own answers. But sometimes, it was just too darn difficult to hold the light while performing surgery on yourself. Time to call for back-up.

They walked down the hall to Ania's massage room. "Do you want me sunny side up or sunny side down?" Raven joked.

"Up." Ania was all business.

Raven stretched out, face up, on the massage table. Ania scanned her body briefly, using her hand like a metal detector at the airport.

"Yep. It's in your throat and right here." Ania poked Raven in the belly. "Let's have a look."

Raven took a deep breath and relaxed into the table. She felt tremendous warmth coming from Ania's hands as she placed one hand near her throat and another on her abdomen.

"What has happened?" Ania asked. "What is *here?*" Ania pressed more firmly, bringing Raven's awareness into her body.

Raven wasn't sure yet.

"I don't know, but I'm hearing those bells they ring at the cathedral down the street. I remember they were ringing and I was noticing a tickle in my throat right when you sent me that e-mail."

"Go on...How did you feel when you heard the bells?"

"Well, I had just been looking at the books on my bookshelf. And I was thinking about how I had started out as such hard-core Christian, you know? I used to be the one who went out to the New Age fairs to try to set people straight!" Raven chuckled.

"And then what?" Ania prodded.

"Well, I had this experience when I was younger. I had been praying and was just overcome with this incredible feeling of light, of oneness. It was pure bliss. I spent my whole life trying to reconnect to what I experienced."

"And now you do it all the time." Ania added.

Raven smiled. "Yes. But wanting to find God, wanting that personal connection, it sent me off in directions the people I knew from church didn't understand. They didn't approve. I would get these looks, you know...

"There was always some person who was well versed in doctrine and what was 'right' trying to set me straight. Here I was learning to listen to my heart to discern truth, and some 'expert' was quoting scripture.

"The heart is deceptive above all things."

"The Ego, sure. But the Heart? Doesn't seem right to me..."

"Like you at the New Age Fairs." Ania brought her back to the point.

"Touché. Yeah. There was this war going on inside me. I guess there still is. Part of me wants more than anything to experience love and oneness with the Divine. The other part wants to be 'OK'. You know, feel like I'm doing the right thing."

"So what is the right thing?" Ania shifted the position of her

Scene Eight: Regression

hands and held them directly over Raven's heart.

"Being loving. Being love. Isn't that what Paul said to the Corinthians? Isn't that supposed to be the whole point? 'Even if I speak with the tongues of angels and cast out demons but have not love I am a clanging gong or clashing cymbal?'" Raven was getting agitated, although a bit impressed she still could spout scripture on demand.

"Uh-huh. So are you?"

"Am I what?"

"Are you love?"

"Well, more than I used to be I guess. At least, I am more loving towards others. I'm more compassionate to myself..."

"And how are you doing with the people from your church?"

Raven did not know what to say. Under the influence of all the light streaming through Ania's hands, she was left with no choice but the truth.

"I don't see much of them anymore." she replied.

"And why not? Since when is separation loving?"

"Because I am afraid of being judged. I am afraid they will tell me I am wrong and that I am doing heretical things. I am afraid they will try to make me stop. I am afraid they will..."

Raven couldn't say it. Ania poked her slender finger in deeper. The pain was excruciating.

"This is very old. This is much deeper. Say it. What do you see? What do you *feel*?"

Raven felt through the darkness for a handle on this deep unnameable fear.

She could feel her heart pumping harder, hear the blood coursing in her ears. Suddenly out of the darkness, a scene faded into view and she was looking down at her own feet on a stone courtyard. Raven looked up and saw that she was standing in what appeared to be the Vatican, several centuries ago. She distinctly heard the sound of bells ringing in the distance.

Stepping through a portico in the wall in front of her strode a group of clerics shoulder to shoulder. They walked in the kind of slow motion Raven once experienced in an auto accident. Their long robes swished side to side. Their rosaries and crucifixes dangling from long beaded chains swung with the rhythm of each step. Raven saw the glare of disdain in the eyes of the one in the middle dressed in red.

They were coming for her.
She had been caught.
They knew.
Someone had told them.

On the table, Raven's body grew ice cold like she had fallen through the ice into a frozen pond. She trembled like a person in the throes of hypothermia. Ania grabbed several blankets and quickly threw them on.

"What has happened now?" she asked.

"They have put me on the stake! Oh dear God! I'm going to be burned at the *freaking* stake!" Raven pulled the blankets tight around her neck, shivering.

"I can feel the wood against my hands... the ropes so tight around my chest I can barely breathe... the smell of the smoke... "

Raven coughed as she tried to clear her throat.

"Oh, God... Please... don't let this happen..."
It's getting hotter. I can smell my own burning flesh."

Raven continued to shiver as her eyes welled up with heavy tears. Her ears filled with her tears as they poured down her cheeks.

"I am looking out into the crowd gathered to witness my death. There is a woman wearing a scarf over her head. She is watching. She is praying for me... She knows what I know."

"And what did you know?" Ania asked.

"I knew how to connect with the Divine directly. I didn't need the priests or the nuns or the rituals to experience Divine love. I could feel it and connect to it on my own. I think I shared that information with the wrong people at the time!"

"Evidently." Ania added with a hint of sarcasm. "What happened next?"

"I don't know. I think I died."

"But after that. What happened?"

"I am still there. I'm like a spirit or something. My soul has

Scene Eight: Regression

stepped out of my charred body and is looking at it, just hanging there, at least what's left of it. And now I am moving through the crowd as they begin to disband.

I can hear their conversations. Some were mortified. Some were sympathetic. Plenty thought I deserved it.

"And what did you think?" Ania inquired.

"I was afraid I had done something terribly wrong. I was afraid to go home. I thought God would completely reject me."

Raven sobbed until her chest was heaving on the table. (Ania bought tissue by the boxcar just for her, she was sure.) Right on cue, the tissue box was laid on her stomach. Ania waited until she was ready to continue.

"So then what? Did she go to the Light?"

"No. She was too afraid. She just stayed here."

"You need to help her go to the Light. Reassure her. Let her know it's OK. Go to her as you are now and give her a hug."

Raven imagined herself walking up to this lost soul and embracing her. She told her it was OK. She let her know it was safe.

She assured her that God would greet her and embrace her with complete unconditional love. She demonstrated how to breathe in the Light until it filled her entire body. Raven watched as the lost soul breathed in the Light and began to slowly disappear. Soon only a blissful smile remained. As the woman's spirit collapsed into a ball of pure white light, Raven felt a huge surge of joy.

"Very good." Ania concluded as she felt the same joy wash over her as well.

"So, Raven, who was judging?"

"Well, *they were!* Those righteous zealots! Where do they get off setting a person on fire because they talk to God? Isn't that what they wanted for people?"

Ania repeated herself, *"Who was judging?"*

Raven looked terribly confused. Had she missed something?

"When you got to the point of returning to the Light, you didn't believe you deserved to go home... So, who was judging?"

"Oh, crap." Raven's eyes flashed with recognition. *"I was!"*

Raven had that look of pure disbelief that Ania relished.

"I will go make some tea. You are good for now. Write this down in that journal of yours." Ania left the room for the kitchen.

Still shivering from all the energy she had discharged, Raven got up from the table and then collapsed into Ania's living room couch. She pulled the blankets all around her and sipped tea until her body found its way back to this place, this time.

It had been a long time since Raven had considered the dilemma she faced whenever she experienced a regression. Her experience on the table was at odds with what she had been taught by official doctrine.

The concept of "past lives" had been embraced by every other spiritual discipline she had ever studied. There was also the theory that these experiences were "genetic memories" held from her ancestors. Another popular concept was that in a quantum universe everything was happening all at once and an individual soul could be present in multiple dimensions or "times."

Whatever the explanation, she recognized that she could never prove any of it. Although she found it interesting that she often knew things about places and times she had never visited or studied only to have them validated later.

Regardless, these symbolic expressions had much to teach her. Just as dreams could unlock deeper meanings through symbol and metaphor, her sessions were equally evocative. She needed to get this down before the lesson began to fade.

Flipping open her journal, Raven wrote:

For years I have felt like I needed to hide, afraid to speak my truth. I am seeing that this fear comes from judgment and separation. I was afraid of judgment from others, and there was a time when that could certainly end badly. Today, I am free to find the Divine for myself, to experience love in my own way, to walk my own path.

I see now that I am the one who is judging. I have been judging myself and I have actually been judging the people I was afraid were judging me. "Forgive us our trespasses as

Scene Eight: Regression

we forgive those who trespass against us." I will keep my focus on love, on connecting with heart, and stop worrying about what other people think.

I also see that I am projecting my own fears of not being right, of not being good enough, on others and the Divine. When I embody love, there is no one who stands against me.

Raven remembered the focus of her original meditations when she first attended a workshop in this room. "I surrender. I trust. I accept." Seemed like a good time to practice.

Scene Nine

Bennu

Wednesday morning meant coffee with Bennu. Raven awoke to Isis doing her kitty yoga on the foot of the bed. Isis arched her back, then kneaded her favorite blanket before snuggling back to sleep. As Isis' yoga mat of choice, the bed offered easy access. Raven had set her simple futon and black wood frame hovering just inches from the bamboo wood floor.

A soft morning breeze lifted gauzy white curtains along the floor, nudging the fabric against the bed frame like a foamy tide rolling in upon a solitary pier. Light streamed through the windows across the stretched out study in relaxation that was Isis in repose.

Raven took her cue from Isis and went through her morning qi gong routine before hitting the shower. As the steam billowed up around her and the warm water cascaded down, Raven reflected about her session two days ago with Ania. She thought about what form the "other shoe" would take as it fell.

It seemed that every time she had an insight on the table, life would present her with a very tangible opportunity to practice in "real life" whatever she thought she understood in the virtual reality world of a session.

Raven wondered if Bennu would deliver today's lesson, or

if something completely unexpected would show up.

Either way, Raven had noticed that over the last seven years, and the last year in particular, the gap between "cause" and "effect" had diminished. These were not the times to spit into the wind unless you wanted to get wet.

Down on the sidewalk in front of her steps, Raven looked as though she had stepped out of the REI Summer Catalog. A forest green sleeveless cotton polo and multi-pocketed khaki capris with draw string legs were finished off with leather hiking sandals. Raven dressed mostly for comfort, but secretly she liked to feel prepared for an adventure at any moment.

The only remarkable accessory that betrayed her artistic side was the pendant she wore designed by her friend, Bennu. Several months ago, she had asked Bennu to create something unique just for her.

Bennu was able to "tune-up" to a person with jewelry design in the same way Raven did with symbols. The outcome was an other-worldly shard of moldavite, cradled by a beautifully sculpted feminine hand cast in silver. Surrounding the dark green leaf-shaped moldavite were tendrils of silver with a black onyx peeking from behind like a distant new moon.

It had taken Raven several months to adapt to the powerful energy of the moldavite amulet, but now they were old friends. The piece seemed to pull her like a magnet towards her best and highest self. It was like a portal into Raven's future potential, each day closing the gap by subtle increments.

Raven hoped that in some way it would be helpful in boosting her intuitive abilities and in revealing the purpose of the symbol she had received in meditation. She needed to know what on Earth she was supposed to do with it.

Raven stopped to empty her mailbox before walking the two blocks to Old Soul. She stuffed an assortment of envelopes and junk mail into a side pocket of her messenger bag, set off across L Street, crossed through the parking lot, and turned the corner onto the cobblestone alleyway.

Raven arrived at the front entrance and looked through the

Scene Nine: Bennu

glass doors to see that her favorite artist buddy, Bennu, was already inside. She was checking out this month's gallery featured on the long brick wall.

Raven could spot her a mile away. It was not just her expressive, artistic manner of dressing, it was Bennu's innate and powerful energy.

Today she wore a pair of soft grey leggings, a vibrant deep red tunic, and her well-worn leather sandals. The carefully orchestrated ensemble was crowned with a surprising nod to practicality — a black denim ball cap attempting to capture Bennu's long dark brown bird's nest of hair. Tendrils of hair escaped in random places giving her an air of, "I don't care what you think, this is working for *me*."

Always accessorized, Bennu was wearing a large silver ankh pendant she had set off with a buffalo bone and turquoise beaded lariat. This combination worked with the solitary earring in her right ear, a striking red hawk feather.

Raven knew that every piece always had a backstory. Some of them she had heard, and some would be a good topic for today's conversation.

"Hey there!" Raven greeted Bennu as she entered. Bennu turned from a large canvas she was studying. She never knew when inspiration might strike for one of her jewelry pieces. Sometimes it was a color, a texture, a theme. Sometimes it just helped her make fresh connections with her own muse. The care and feeding of the creative process was familiar to Raven as well.

Raven greeted her friend with a hug.

Bennu seemed to tolerate her hugs, even though Raven suspected she could just as easily pass if Raven were to forget.

"You already order?" Raven inquired.

"Yep. Latte, add shot. My usual."

Raven stepped over to the counter and placed her order.

"Iced Americano today. It's still too warm for the hot stuff."

Raven joined Bennu in facing the wall and studied the paintings while waiting for their orders.

"This one is amazing." Bennu pointed out. "What do you see here?"

"I really like the textures. Kind of reminds me of embossed handmade paper. Do you think you could translate that effect into metal? I bet it would make an awesome piece." Raven concluded.

Bennu nodded, her eyes following every curve and contour. Raven could tell she was already mentally in the studio running metal through her press and deciding what else to do with it.

They were interrupted by the voice from the service counter.

"Latte, extra shot! Iced Americano!"

The artists picked up their drinks and without needing to discuss the matter went looking for a table outside.

Scene Ten

Galactic Underworld

Raven liked the conversational shortcuts offered by social media. She found she didn't have to waste an hour getting caught up with surface level details. She could just go straight for the juicy stuff behind the status updates.

"So, what have you been working on lately? I saw that post on Facebook that linked to your blog... the one about your doodles and dreams."

"Oh, yeah, lots of stuff came out of that dream. The cracked goblet, the chrysanthemum and the snake.... I was doing tendrils and vines on stuff for weeks! But what I'm really excited about lately is *this* one." To give Raven a better look, Bennu held out the silver ankh pendant from around her neck.

"You know, I've always been totally fascinated with ancient Egypt. When I was about eight, I devoured just about everything I could get my hands on from the *Worldbook Encyclopedia* in my Dad's den. My favorite volume was 'E'. Eagle. Easter. Egypt."

Even at eight, I wasn't quite buyin' the Worldbook version on the history of the holiday.

Made me a real pain at the annual Episcopal church egg hunt. Too bad I didn't get further with my study of hieroglyphics, though..."

"Why's that?" Raven asked between slurps of iced Americano.

"Had the weirdest dream this last week." Bennu continued. "Well, actually it was that same dream where I saw the wine goblet and the snake that I mentioned on the blog post... there was also this man holding up a cardboard sign. The sign had a message for me in *glyphs*."

"Weird." said Raven. "What do you think it means?"

"Not sure yet. But I'm going to go with the Egyptian symbolism as a theme for awhile and play with it. I'm sure something will surface when I do. It always does." Bennu took a sip of her latte. "So, what's new with you, Raven?"

"Oh. Besides the big barbeque at the Vatican you mean? Raven, *it's what's for dinner!*" she joked, attempting to mask her discomfort. "I got to experience being burned at the stake. I had a seriously crazy regression session up at Ania's."

"Well, at least no one had to eat *crow*." Bennu winked. "I'm pretty sure I have a few of those in my past as well."

"You're just lucky things didn't get out of hand at the Easter egg hunt." Raven chided.

"Anyway, it's really had me thinking." Raven continued. "I've been doing a lot of processing since I got back. Are you familiar with Carl Johan Calleman's book, *The Mayan Calendar and the Transformation of Consciousness?*"

"I'm familiar with the concept, but never read that one in particular. Crazy Mayan Calendar has everybody all worked up right now. I can't tell you how many bizarre theories are running around about what will happen in 2012." Bennu said.

"Tell me about it." Raven agreed. "One group is waiting for the Rapture or the Second Coming. Another group is waiting on aliens to make first contact and bring us new technology to save the planet.

"The least disruptive version involves people awakening overnight to a new level of consciousness and getting our act together before we destroy ourselves. Oh, and then there's the spaceships taking the chosen ones to the parallel new Earth in another dimension. And those are the optimistic ones!" Raven shook her head in disbelief.

"The negative ones are expecting the Earth to reverse its

Scene Ten: Galactic Underworld

poles, solar flares to fry us to a crisp, or the ice caps to melt and create another Great Flood." Bennu said.

"Don't forget the hostile aliens, the giant planet killing caldera or asteroid, or the anti-Christ and the Horsemen of the Apocalypse." Raven added.

"Yes. "Bennu reflected. "It's an equal opportunity apocalypse."

"Have you noticed something they all have in common?" Raven asked. "All of these hysterics are about waiting for something *external* to come and either save us or destroy us.

Who knows… I suspect there are larger forces at work. And perhaps there are other dimensional beings assisting us. As weird as it sounds, I honestly don't doubt that.

But ultimately, I believe that transformation is an *inside* job. Each individual must choose whether they will align with love or with something that is not love."

Bennu reflected, "Come to think of it, maybe all these externals we're waiting for are actually waiting for us. They're waiting for us to get our act together before showing themselves. It's not *their* mess to clean up, it's ours."

"Depending on who you talk to, we just kill or ridicule the prophets of higher consciousness anyway. Why go through *that* all over again? Better to wait until the time is…. right." said Raven.

"Anyway, if you ask me, I think we will look back on this time like we did the millennium and all the hype around Y2K." Raven noted. "Remember all the doom and gloom and the fear mongering? Then it came and went and people just looked at each other and shrugged like "what was all that about?"

"Everybody, *back to work!* Coffee break over! Stop rubber-necking on the evolutionary freeway." Bennu pretended to be directing the traffic of an easily distracted humanity.

" I think it is foolish to pin everything on a single date on the calendar. Who knows? Maybe history will prove me wrong." Raven concluded.

"With everything you've experienced the last few years, do you *not* think it will happen?" Bennu interjected.

"Do I think humanity is on the edge of a huge turning point? Do I believe we are evolving? Yes. Absolutely. But really, I don't think it will happen all at once like a big Hollywood blockbuster movie.

I think it will be more like the American civil rights movement or the spread of technology in the last twenty years. This may happen at a faster pace than those events because the energy currently supports it, but it will still be a *process*.

There will be people who are ahead of the curve—trail blazers and path finders. They will create the environment and set the tone for change. They will show us the way by living it, by embodying it.

Then there will be a critical mass that just makes this new way of living and thinking a part of their everyday lives. No fanfare, just a quiet revolution. Eventually, enough people will have an effect on their friends, families, coworkers, and neighbors that we will accept a more loving, compassionate, connected way of life as the new normal. We will expect it.

Within a couple of generations we will look back at this time and be amazed. We will say, 'Hey, it really *did* start to shift in those years, but not like we thought.' It will be like a young person today not knowing life before the internet or television."

"Yes. The Elders will sit around the holographic fire and tell the stories of when phones with wires could not roam the Earth." Bennu chuckled.

"Or when books were still produced on paper." Raven added.

"Or when people still needed books to know stuff." Bennu was running with it now.

Raven reflected, "I think we may find we need fewer books to know stuff. Maybe there will be a backlash to our current information overload. We may replace books and static information with more conversations and direct experiences.

Haven't you noticed that everything is changing so fast that being current is more about being present than being informed?"

"And then the Artists will rule the Earth!" Bennu raised her arms like she might spike a football and dance in the end zone.

"Yes. We will be benevolent rulers," Raven played along. "Sixty-four crayons in every box and freedom of expression for everyone!"

Scene Ten: Galactic Underworld

They tapped their coffee cups together to seal the evolution revolution. A few moments passed between them as they each smiled and reflected on the juxtaposition of their conversation. Like the work of a court jester, insight had cloaked itself amidst outright silliness.

Finding the thread back to her original thought, Raven continued, "But what I started to say about Calleman is we are supposedly living in what he calls the Galactic Underworld on the Mayan Calendar. The evolution of consciousness has brought humanity to a period of time in which our lessons as a species are all about healing. In particular, healing the issues regarding imbalances in power.

"The hierarchies that have dominated world politics, religion, and how men and women, even adults and children relate to one another are all due for an operating system upgrade, so to speak. We are learning how to be collaborative versus competitive, connected versus controlling... duality is giving way to unity."

While she talked, Raven began to sort through the mail she had picked up on her way out of the apartment that morning. One envelope in particular stood out as odd. It was very official looking. The letter was from the Superior Court System of California. Raven opened it as curiosity danced with fear.

"I don't believe it... " she sat stunned—staring at Bennu and not knowing what to say next.

"What is it?" Bennu leaned forward, expecting the worst.

"This client I did some work for over a year ago is taking me to small claims court!" Raven exclaimed.

Bennu leaned back in her chair. "Well, it appears that Earth school is calling you in to take a little pop quiz. Think you're ready?"

Raven felt the same dread she had felt in her session as the clerics strode through the portico with their determined scowls. She felt herself come up against the same wall of fear— the fear of being trapped. She also felt a misplaced sense of guilt, an uncertainty about the outcome, and a very primal urge to either run or rip this man's head off.

She recognized her anger was a trap door to her fear. And so she wrestled between allowing herself to feel it and wanting it to just go away. Raven didn't want to believe she still had this kind of fear and anger still in her. She had worked too hard to release so much of it.

She sat there just sipping the last drops of her Americano and staring at the ice cubes as they melted. The "other shoe" had fallen, she realized. This was the real world test for the lesson she had learned on the table.

"I've got two weeks before the court date." Raven began folding the letter back up to put in her bag. "Two weeks to prepare."

"Your case?" Bennu asked.

"No." Raven looked pensive. "My heart."

Scene Eleven

Energetic Wisdom

Raven was grateful for work to take her mind off the Superior Court and the "party invitation" she had just pulled from her mailbox. Susan Rueppel at Energetic Wisdom was on her schedule that afternoon, and Raven looked forward to meeting the client they would be consulting.

Raven collected her art supplies—an 11"x14" pad of paper, an assortment of brush tipped markers, and her chalk pastels. Placing them in her messenger bag, she rolled her bike out of the apartment, locking the door behind her.

She had become skilled over the last few months at placing the bike frame on her shoulder as she maneuvered her way down the two sets of stairs to the sidewalk. The ride to Susan's office was just a few blocks away— from 18th and L to 23d and J.

Pedaling through mid-town, Raven thought back to the day just six months ago when she had been Susan's client. If Madame Zelda was a fortune cookie, Susan was more like the Oracle at Delphi.

Her professional office was located in a shared space with an art gallery and a chic hair salon. Full of natural light and walls painted in mid-tone hues of blue and green, Susan's office created an immediate feeling of calm and trust.

Susan herself defied the stereotype for "intuitive types." A petite and spunky blonde always dressed to perfection in stylish business suits, she exuded a bright cheerfulness most evident from the warmth of her generous smile.

Raven found it fascinating that what many people in this field had stumbled into by accident, Susan had cultivated very deliberately and almost academically. She was a diligent student of her art and had the Ph.D. in Esoteric Philosophy and Hermetic Science to prove it.

Among other protocols, Susan was a trained medical intuitive and Raven was curious if there was anything going on in her body she should know about.

Not much, as it turned out. All the action was "other-dimensional." An MP3 recorder on the glass coffee table captured every word of the consultation, and Raven had listened to the recording a dozen times since to make sure she understood its meaning and implications.

As Raven recalled, the consultation had begun with Susan's observation of Raven's energy in and around her auric field. She noticed a yellow hue that represented the recent "illuminating of who you really are" and a turquoise color showing "integration of the spiritual and physical."

What Susan said next still had Raven simultaneously in awe and disbelief:

"I am seeing all this information just zooming in. You are like a magnet for this wisdom and information coming in from other realms. It's like the crystalline structure of your being has recently solidified and you have gone from being like two tin cans with a string between them to this broadband network, this freeway, of information.

"Your life up until now has been about building up to this point where your crystalline structure is complete and able to integrate and bring forth this energy.

"Everything you have done —your spiritual seeking and practice, your graphics and symbol work, your healing work for yourself and others— have all culminated for this core purpose. This is what you have been training for in Earth school in this lifetime. You have been gathering this knowledge and been part of

Scene Eleven: Energetic Wisdom

an exchange of information between our planet and many other spaces and places.

"You are showing us an image of a large brass key-ring... I see you collecting these "keys" and bringing them in from these other realms... What you are bringing forth is not just for humans and not just for this planet. You are integrating them and creating a Universal Master Key.

Now what I am seeing is that you have become the Master Key. You hold that energy and are now physically and energetically an embodiment of the Master Key.

Essentially, what you will be drawing... *is yourself.*"

Raven recalled her own audible gasp on the recording.

Susan continued, "A big part of your soul contract is to bring forward the Master Key and to anchor and ground this energy within your body and within the Earth. Make the energy of Universal Healing manifest."

Raven had spent the last six months in meditation and contemplation "unpacking" what she had learned from Susan. So far, she had intuited the nature and the structure of the symbol. She had asked for Guidance and rendered the image she had recently sent to Ania.

The Master Key symbol itself was a work of sacred geometry, a fractal, similar in appearance to crop circles but in 3D. It contained 12 "rays" wrapped around a sphere like latitude lines on a sphere.

Each ray contained 12 "nodes" like beads on a string. The 12 rays of 12 nodes created a total of 144 nodes in the overall structure. There were 6 nodes above the "equator" and six nodes below it.

The nodes progressed in size consistent with phi (The Divine Proportion or the Fibonacci Sequence): 1,2,3,5,8, and 13. The spacing between the nodes followed a reverse pattern, so that the space between the 1 and 2 was a quantity of 13, while the space between the 8 and 13 was 1.

Each node held an integrated duality of masculine (yang) and feminine (yin) or positive and negative energy, and each one progressed along the spectrum of light through red, orange, yellow, green, blue, to violet.

Essentially, they reflected the chakra system of the multi-verse. The entire structure had a column of pure white light that ran through its core between the north and south poles.

Visually, the symbol communicated volumes to those able to discern its deeper meanings. Raven recognized that it demonstrated the Hermetic principle, "As above, so below" and the connection between "space/time" and "time/space", as well as the integration of the alpha and omega.

Raven's leather bound journal was filled with notes, sketches, and diagrams of what she had learned about the nature of the Master Key since that afternoon in Susan's office.

In six months she had a pretty good idea what it looked like, and she had confirmation that it represented the consciousness she expected, but one nagging question remained.

"What am I supposed to do with it?" Raven could just imagine herself holding a press conference and announcing to the world, "Hellooooo World! I have been in contact with benevolent beings in other realms, and my life purpose is to embody and introduce you to a symbol that integrates the energy of Universal Healing. Here it is! Behold... The Symbol! Please take a good look and report back here tomorrow fully enlightened. Thank you and have a nice day."

In fact, the whole situation was like some comical sequel to The Hitchhiker's Guide to the Galaxy. Rather than a supercomputer named Deep Thought pondering the Answer to the Ultimate Question of Life, the Universe, and Everything and coming up with "42", Raven had apparently scoured the universe for the Universal Master Keys of Healing and come up with a symbol you could stick on a coaster and upgrade your level of consciousness.

Raven had decided to wait a bit before sharing this with anyone she still wanted to regard her as sane. On the off chance there was something to it (and the Universe was indeed counting on her) she remained on the alert for additional information.

Over the last six months she experienced a variety of thoughts and emotions. She had been at turns incredulous, intoxicated with grandiosity, in and out of disbelief, lowered to the depths of humility, and generally just overwhelmed with the whole concept.

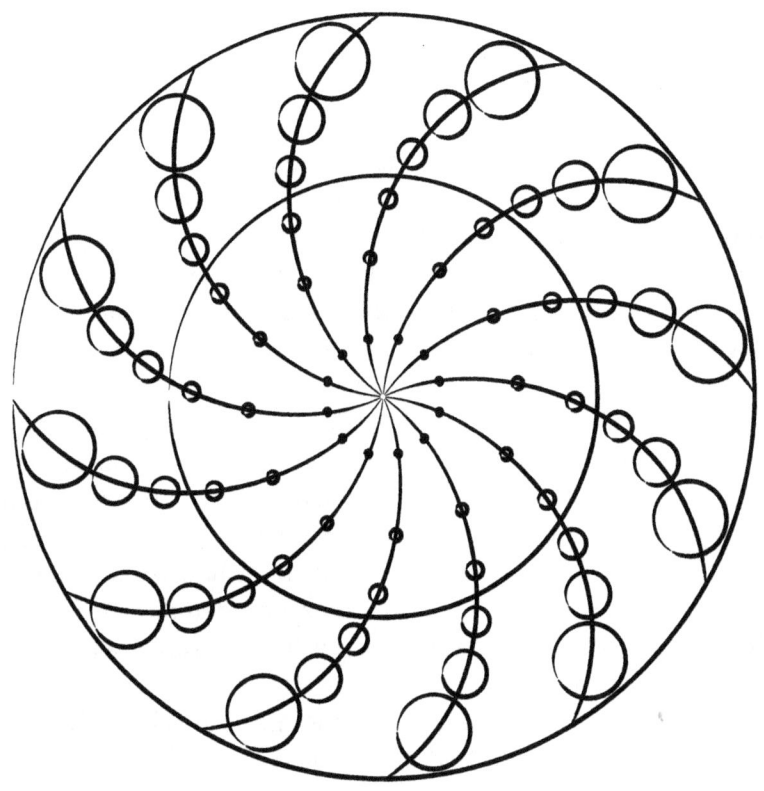

Master Key structure depicting the Key from the perspective of the bottom looking up. This is one half of the total structure. The other "hemisphere" rotates in the opposite direction.

Raven conceded that if only one random card reader had mentioned her "great task", she might have shrugged it off years ago. What nagged at her was the continuity of the information and the fact that it relentlessly came from different sources over many years.

The information contained greater levels of specificity each time until Susan had spelled it out completely.

Raven found it hard to ignore that she had effortlessly intuited the symbol within a few days, and that Ania had just confirmed it's energetic vibration. Without hearing anything about how or why Raven had created it, Ania had identified that it resonated with the Galactic Level of Consciousness as described by Calleman. It was a "visual tuning fork" for love, healing, and unity.

Over the last few months, Raven had thought a lot about the people she had admired throughout history— the saints, the artists, the activists, the revolutionaries, the visionary scientists and inventors. All of them, at one time, held a "dangerous" or outrageous perception of reality. Most of them had come up against people who thought them either crazy or delusional. She wondered if she had the courage to step into their ranks and play out this improbable destiny.

What kept her going was imagining herself on "the other side" as a soul who had died and moved on to The Light. What if she had been given a gift and not used it, given information and ignored it, given the opportunity and squandered it, and given support and refused it? If she really *did* have an important role to play in the symphony of humanity, she wanted to come in on cue and play it to the best of her ability.

Raven had willingly "downloaded" the symbol, she had accepted her role as the embodiment and communicator of the symbol, but she just couldn't seem to comprehend how she was supposed to "bring it forward" and gift it to the world. She ached for some new information to present itself while she worked with Susan this afternoon.

Parking her bike and locking it to the bike rack out front, she threw her messenger bag full of art supplies over her shoulder and crossed the threshold of Energetic Wisdom.

Scene Twelve

Soul Prints

Energetic Wisdom was the name of Susan's intuitive consulting business. Raven and Susan offered a collaborative service where they each did their own type of intuitive reading for the same client.

An "intuitive duet," Susan presented intuitive answers to the client's business questions while Raven drew out a symbolic representation of the client's situation she called a Soul Print.

Raven explained to clients that it was like getting two different maps of the same terrain, like a topographic map and street map of the same square mile.

Raven greeted Susan with a hug and began to set up her work space before their client arrived. She set her art supplies on a small table across the room from Susan's desk—preparing the art paper, the brush markers, and the chalk pastels to have them in easy reach as needed.

Today's client was a small business owner looking to sort out a myriad of opportunities and make an informed decision about where to put her focus for the next few months.

Clarity was the key benefit their clients were after. The small business owners Raven knew resembled weary travelers returning from an extended business trip only to discover all the locks had been changed on their doors. The current business climate was unpredictable at best and perilous at worst. The "sure thing" strategies of just a few years ago weren't working like they used to in today's economy.

Business owners needed every advantage they could get, and some of them were learning that intuition was the one place they may not have taken a serious look that could still produce some gold.

Susan walked their client, Marjorie, through a preliminary orientation. She explained the paperwork, the protocol, what Raven was doing on the side, and asked for the client's permission to access their energy via their birth name.

She invited Marjorie to ask her first question. Marjorie explained that her business was stuck. She had been putting in insane hours and finding less and less return for her efforts. More than ever, she could not afford to make an expensive mistake in trying something new.

She had a number of potential opportunities, but wondered which ones (if any) were worth the time, money, and effort needed to develop them.

Susan began her response to Marjorie's questions and made notes with drawings as she spoke. Raven was listening to them in the background, like she would notice music playing in a room where she was working. She was not drawing directly from what Susan was saying, however.

Raven waited for the moment when a picture would fully form in her mind. She had learned from practice that all she had to do was ask, and it would show up right on cue.

Raven used the same method in her work she used in meditation. Taking a deep breath, she relaxed and said to herself, "I invite the Light... please guide me."

Raven saw in her mind's eye the image of an English "turnabout" intersection where cars entered from multiple directions and flowed around the circle until they turned off to the intended avenue to exit and continue their journey.

Scene Twelve: Soul Prints

Nothing Susan had said yet seemed to support this, but Raven went with her own intuition anyway.

Raven reached for a purple brush marker, then a bright green one, then an orange marker, and finally a red one. There were four avenues that branched out from the turn-about, each with their own distinct color. Raven paused and waited for Marjorie to tell them more about her business.

"So, right now I have really four options I'm looking at…"

Raven smiled to herself. In her mind, Raven thought, "Yes you do… and they each take you in completely different directions but they will dance around with each other for awhile…"

Marjorie continued, "I could keep doing what I'm doing. I could sell the business to my partner and go do something else. I could work on developing a new line of services and presenting that to our current market, or I could take our current services and introduce them to a completely different market."

"What do you think makes the most sense right now?" Marjorie asked Susan. While Susan answered her question, Raven again turned to her own Guidance.

Raven saw that if Marjorie kept doing what she was doing, it would take her down the avenue that was drawn in red. This was a dead end and she would probably find herself metaphorically out of gas and without cell signal to call the tow truck. Raven drew in a little cautionary yellow sign on the red street that said, "Dead End."

Next Raven felt the energy of the purple avenue and recognized that it represented selling the business to her partner. She saw this as a possibility, but a small one. Her partner was probably not in a position financially to buy the business outright and Marjorie would have to start completely over. She would either have to build another business from scratch or get a job. Either way, she would not be doing what she was truly passionate about and would probably regret it.

Raven drew a sign that said, "For Sale" in purple with a series of plants along the purple road that progressively wilted, then died off. Raven wondered why this street was purple, then the image of a bruise came to mind. "Be careful, you might get bruised or beat up on this route" she noted.

Observing the emerging picture, Raven focused on the green and orange avenues. The green avenue represented "new growth" like fresh Spring grass. To her surprise, this green path needed to split into two smaller paths. One path represented taking her existing services to new markets, while the other represented introducing new services to her existing customer base.

Raven made a note on each one and drew customers wearing T-shirts standing along each route. One group wore shirts that said,"NEW" while the other group wore shirts that said, "NOW." Raven was pleased she avoided labeling them as "old" customers.

The only road that remained a mystery was the orange one. Raven focused her awareness to discover what it could represent. "Why orange?"

Immediately, she saw in her mind's eye a blazing bonfire. The orange flames danced and swayed with powerful energy, extending themselves up and illuminating the faces of many people standing around the fire.

"Marjorie needs to unleash something she is very passionate about and hasn't shared yet with the world." Raven thought. She drew a bonfire at the end of this orange road and a sign at its beginning that read "Your Passion."

Raven listened to the reading in progress with Susan for any salient details that might further illuminate the symbols Raven was seeing for Marjorie.

"And what is coming forward next is that you are burying some of your gifts and talents because you don't believe there is a market for them..." Susan stated as she drew on her consultation sheet a grave with a headstone that read R.I.P.

"Bingo!" thought Raven. It was always fun to see how they would each tap into their own source of knowing and pull out similar information, yet represent it in their own unique ways.

The closest comparison Raven could relate these intuitive sessions to was when she played the flute in symphonic band in high school. She remembered what it was like to be listening to the other players as they entered and fell away according to their parts. She had to focus on the mastery of her individual instrument, know

Scene Twelve: Soul Prints

her part, and watch the conductor for timely cues.

The thing Raven liked most about symphonic music was the joy it created inside when everything was in harmony and the music was greater than the people making it—as if it had a soul of its own.

This state of "flow" that was integral to creative endeavors and heightened by intuitive guidance made it about the most enjoyable way to make a living Raven could possibly imagine.

As the session progressed, Raven added details, filled in the segments with pastel color blocks to distinguish the differing paths, and listened intuitively for other distinctions that would be helpful to the client later.

When nothing else flowed through her intuitive pipeline, Raven signed her work and dated it. She put away her materials and prepared to present the drawing to Marjorie.

As Raven stepped forward and placed the large sheet of paper in front of her client, Marjorie's eyes lit up as they darted from place to place in the illustration to take it all in.

Susan smiled from across the desk as she recognized the themes they had been discussing in their session, and that Raven had shown them in a different yet integrated way.

The two of them had noticed a pattern over their many sessions. Susan's consultation took the client from where they were when they stepped in the door to where they most desired to go but probably couldn't articulate or imagine.

Raven would immediately see a symbol that summed up the crux or theme of the issue, but if she had told the client what she saw, it would have totally confused them because they were not yet ready to hear it.

Together, they created a powerful multi-sensory experience that created a new level of clarity for each client and empowered them to move forward with confidence in the days and weeks to come.

Marjorie thanked them and wrote out her check.

She left with a big smile and a renewed sense of self confidence. She had a revised map of her world and she was eager to get out and explore it.

Raven turned to Susan as Marjorie headed out the door towards J Street. "That was fun..." Raven smiled. "As always."

"Sure was." Susan agreed.

As Raven packed up her pens and pastels and helped Susan put the table back into her storage closet, she thought this might be a good time to get a second opinion.

"You know that Master Key project? Well, I'm getting an intuition that I need to go and ground this energy somewhere. I'm thinking I'm due for at least three days in Yosemite..."

Susan paused before responding. Raven recognized when an intuitive was checking something besides their own opinions.

"Yep. That sounds about right. I'm surprised it took you this long!" Susan said with a wink. Raven gave Susan a hug and thanked her for the nudge.

Raven had been feeling a sense of urgency lately. She needed to focus and have plenty of quiet time in nature to get clear on what she was supposed to do next. Most especially, what she was supposed to do with the symbol.

If the Universe was threatening to put someone else in the game, she at least wanted a chance to talk to the Head Coach and study the play book.

The energy in Yosemite was big, nurturing, feminine. It was a very powerful place to ground an equally powerful and healing energy.

As Raven looked at her calendar to book a reservation from her phone, she realized that the weekend she needed to be there would include Sunday. The date would be 10-10-10.

SECTION TWO

DOWN TO EARTH

Scene Thirteen

THE BUG

"Passion." That was the word Raven wrote by the blazing bonfire near the orange path on Marjorie's Soul Print.

She was reminded of that image and this vital word as she watched the orange and yellow flames cavorting in the large stone fireplace inside the Yosemite Bug Cafe. The light from the fireplace created a soothing ambient glow throughout the rustic lodge dining area.

Antique skis, snowshoes, sleds and other mountain memorabilia decorated the pine log walls and overhead beams to give this place a feeling that was somewhere between a ski lodge and a college dorm common area.

"Passion" to Raven meant taking decisive action on whatever really mattered in her heart. As long as Raven could remember, she had always felt a passionate desire to connect. She sought to connect with the Divine, with the depths of her being, with other people. Raven also sought to make connections between ideas and between "worlds."

Looking back, her feet had straddled the line between worlds since birth. She was a child of both the East and the West and yet never really fit with either.

She was born the very last year of the Baby Boom and was

identified by market researchers as a "cusper"— neither Boomer nor a solid citizen of Generation X. Her Chinese horoscope placed her within several days of being either a Dragon or a Rabbit.

Her Mayan sun sign placed her within hours of being a Jaguar (Ix) or a Cane (Ben). The Jaguar was the inter-dimensional shape shifter, the sun runner, the magician. Cane was rooted in the earth and connected the worlds of above and below.

No matter the map, the symbolism was the same—one "above" and the other "below." Somehow she was always integrating the two. Even the moldavite pendant around her neck was a melding of meteorite and planet Earth.

If anyone knew what it felt like to be connected to everything and belong to nothing in particular it was Raven. She puzzled over the fact that she could so easily read the core essence of another human being, feel deeply connected on a soul level, yet still find herself out of step with much of the world around her.

Part of what made it possible for Raven to navigate her "dual citizenship" was maintaining openness. She was pleased at how nimble she had been to arrange the next three days in Yosemite.

A quick call to Bennu arranged food and attention for Isis for the week. Three days in a tent cabin were reserved online within five minutes. It was easy. She had been to the Bug, an international hostel, many times before and held a yearly park pass for Yosemite.

With October being "off season" and her traveling alone, she had no problem finding a cabin for the following weekend. The reservation desk had assigned her an insulated plywood cabin high up on the hill. Her cabin was designated Chilnualna 'D' (named for the falls in the park), and when Raven walked up to unpack she had to smile when the stick-on letters on the dark green front door simply spelled "CHIL D."

In every way, Raven sought the nurturing and maternal support of this place to get her bearings and keep moving forward. The room assignment seemed to confirm that here she could lean into the loving arms of grace and trust. Raven chuckled to herself as she thought, "The Child can chill."

Looking around the Cafe, she remembered how much she

Scene Thirteen: The Bug

enjoyed the variety of visitors she saw there. She overheard lively conversations in Japanese, German, Swedish, Spanish, and English.

She glanced around to see men and women with backpacks in their mid-twenties checking their e-mail on the cafe computer or referring to topographic maps spread out on the table to plan their hikes for the next day.

Families with children played board games and put puzzles together as they laughed and told stories from their adventures in the park that day.

A retired couple sipped coffee as they reviewed their favorite photos on their digital camera.

"I'm so glad we bought that macro lens before our trip" the husband said. "The colors are fantastic, don't you think?"

His wife smiled and nodded, looking at him with a softness and a delight created by decades of appreciating life's little blessings in between the big events and minor tragedies.

Raven wondered how many trips they had taken together.

How many photos from trips like this one filled picture frames and thick albums with sticky-backed, peel-away plastic pages in their den? How many memories had they woven in and out of everyday moments sipping coffee, grocery shopping, watching television, maybe tending a garden, or watching the sun set in their backyard.

Watching the couple, Raven thought about her relationship with Alex. They were "on a break" for now. Their relationship needed some space as they were each wrestling with their priorities.

On one hand, Alex was her undisputed soulmate. He was intelligent, good-looking, well-informed about a variety of topics, and deep down had a heart of gold.

Alex would hand five dollars to a homeless person if he had only ten bucks in his wallet. On the other hand, there was baggage.

They had attempted to start a business together and nothing had worked the way they hoped. They both invested a lot of time and money, and each had very different ideas about what they wanted from the business.

The stress of the business revealed the fractures within their relationship. Old wounds eroded their trust. Blame and bitterness always resurfaced whenever they tried to move forward. Raven hoped they could start fresh one day, but wasn't sure what kind of miracle it would take to reconcile all that hurt.

Deep down, Raven believed in "soul contracts"— the idea that certain key people were in her life by prior agreement.

Alex felt like an old friend from the minute they met. Most of the lessons in her life that stretched her always involved him. Raven often thought he must love her tremendously to show up on schedule and serve up such heart-wrenching and life changing lessons. She valued him in her life, but questioned their future.

The gap between what she believed to be true about love and the real life practice of acceptance, forgiveness, authenticity, and genuine intimacy was a constant challenge.

"It is one thing to talk about love as an ideal, and quite another to live it—to embody it." she thought.

The coolness of autumn had settled in to the mountains in a way that had not yet touched Sacramento. Raven enjoyed the cozy feel of her soft cotton mock-turtle neck, fleece pull-over, and baggy grey sweat pants.

She looked over the tops of her hiking boots kicked up on coffee table in front of the fire and thought about her plan for the next three days.

Tonight she got settled, ate dinner, and meditated on what to do over the next few days. Tomorrow she would hike the Mist Trail and meditate at Vernal Falls, placing her near Half Dome on 10-10-10. After that, she would see where Spirit led her—perhaps somewhere in the valley, perhaps the redwood grove.

She had always wanted to visit the 2700 year old tree that was the treasure of the Sequoia Grove on the southern tip of the park.

Raven kept her plans on these adventures sketchy. Listening, receiving, and allowing were the rhythm of choice for the next few days. Raven stood and gathered her journal and pen.

Switching on her flashlight, she climbed the winding wood plank steps up the hillside to CHIL-D.

SCENE FOURTEEN

Good Morning, Sunshine

Raven was teased awake by the smell of coffee and bacon blowing in on a soft breeze from the Cafe down the hill.

With one eye barely open, she noticed the sunlight streaming through the small cloth curtains covering sliding glass windows no bigger than open school books. Outside the window she heard bird song mixed with human voices.

She heard one group of car doors open and shut while another group of car engines turned over and revved up the hill to the exit. Heavy footsteps echoed up the hillside as people hiked up and down the wooden plank steps under the weight of luggage and camping gear.

Raven pulled the edge of her sleeping bag up around her neck and rolled over onto her side. The October air was creating a bit of a chill that made the sleeping bag she packed seem like an especially good idea.

Scanning her room in the light of day, Raven noted that this was definitely a no frills arrangement for people who really just needed a place to stay the night in between visits to Yosemite National Park. Her simple cabin furnishings included a small double bed with a mattress and metal bed frame, two small plywood cabinets to store clothing, and a couple of plastic lawn chairs. She could have rented something more full-featured, but decided she would rather stay longer for the same budget. Reasonably comfortable, the cabin had a space heater and was just a short walk to a shared restroom down the hill.

At this point, the battle began between her body and her soul. Her body needed to visit the restroom and go in search of that alluring coffee and bacon and her spirit wanted to meditate, do some qi gong in front of the cabin, and write in her journal.

The battle went to the bladder and bacon.

Raven threw on her sweats and sandals, grabbed a small bag with her key, wallet, and toothbrush and headed out the door into the embrace of fresh morning mountain air filled with the scent of pine. She took a deep breath and savored the fragrance as her feet crunched pine needles and dry grass on her way down the embankment.

Creating her own noisy cadence of footsteps for some other camper to awaken to, she worked her way down the plank steps to the Cafe. Raven decided today would be her day to hike the Mist Trail to Vernal Falls. She could not imagine a more meaningful place for her to ground the Master Key energy, or a better place to be on 10-10-10.

As she ordered her breakfast and waited for it to arrive, she thought about the last time she had hiked the Mist Trail and how that climb to Vernal Falls had dramatically changed her life.

Scene Fifteen

Vernal Falls

It was 2008 and Raven was here with a group of women friends for a long weekend. All Raven had wanted to do that weekend was be a plain brown paper bag of a person.

She didn't want to talk about spiritual things or psychological things. She didn't want to be "deep." She didn't want to have the kind of crazy "woo woo" conversations she had with friends like Bennu. She didn't want to do anything but be "one of the girls" and talk about the simple, mundane, everyday things that girlfriends (she had heard) talk about when they get together. Raven just wanted to laugh a lot, enjoy nature and make some new friends. That is exactly how the weekend had gone until "The Vernal Falls Incident."

Raven was among six middle-aged women friends who set out before noon to hike the Mist Trail. For the first hour, they lumbered up the paved pathway that gradually increased in steepness and altitude to the foot bridge at the base of the falls.

They paused often to take pictures, rest breaks, and sip water. Every one of them was enthralled with the beauty and the grandeur of the scenery and the intimacy of their conversations. Over the next hour and a half, they progressed further up to the treacherous slippery rock passage and became soaked with water gushing off the falls from the abundant Spring run-off.

Everything appeared to be going well as they took pictures, laughed and talked in smaller groups of twos and threes as they hiked along. Three of them, including Raven, made it to the top first and started to prepare their picnic lunch. The other three women were taking a very long time and arrived at the top of Vernal Falls nearly 40 minutes later.

Raven would never forget the scene. Dragging herself on hands and knees through the mud was Rachel. She could hardly get her body to cooperate in putting one foot in front of the other.

Rachel made it through the narrow pass by herself by crawling. Once through the passage, Nan and Linda came alongside her on each side for support. Her legs had completely "locked up" in spasm and she could not move on her own.

Each woman held on to Rachel's waist, her hand grasping Rachel's belt for a stronger grip. Rachel draped her arms over their shoulders.

The scene looked like something enacted by countless soldiers on the field of battle—two exhausted buddies carrying a wounded friend out of the line of fire.

Only this scene was at the crest of a spectacular waterfall, three-hundred feet above the river below. These were not soldiers, but soaked and exhausted middle-aged women on a weekend camping trip.

Upon seeing their friends cresting the ridge, Raven and the two others, Meshell and Olivia, dropped everything and ran to help.

"What happened?!" They all gasped in unison.

"It's my fibromyalgia," Rachel said. "Don't worry. I brought some of my medication. It should clear up with some rest." Nan and Linda set her down on a rock to rest and find her medication. Rachel fumbled with the zipper of her backpack, then rummaged through every compartment, twice, for her pills.

The group of women seemed suspended in time as the sound of the crashing water and fine spray washed over them. Not seeing anything useful emerge from the bag, they collectively held their breath and feared the worst.

Scene Fifteen: Vernal Falls

"It's not in here." Rachel looked stunned.

Rachel's words triggered everything in Raven's perception to slow down and focus. She felt a wave of dread as she imagined them all carrying Rachel down the slippery jagged rock steps, or needing to get a Life Flight helicopter to bring her friend safely down the mountain.

Apparently, every other woman in the group thought the same thing. At this point, Raven's intuitive Guidance came knocking.

"You need to help her," a small voice spoke from within.

"Oh... please. Not here. Not now!" Raven had thought. She did not want to be "weird." She did not want to draw a lot of attention to herself and she sure didn't want to have to explain any of this to anyone.

Raven knew what Guidance wanted her to do. In her mind's eye, she saw herself working on Rachel on a nearby rock and doing a similar kind of session to what she had learned from Ania at workshops. She knew the roar of the waterfall was too great to have a conversation with Rachel, so she would have to do something different than what she had experienced before.

The other fear gripping Raven was *"What if it doesn't work? What if I expose myself as a total nut-burger and it doesn't even help?"* Still looking for a way out, Raven offered Rachel an ibuprofen.

As Rachel threw back three ibuprofen with some water and thanked Raven for the effort, Nan volunteered to massage Rachel's legs to see if it would help. They moved Rachel over to the rock Raven had already seen in her intuition, laid out a small blanket, and Nan went to work kneading Rachel's tense legs.

Raven was once more nudged by her Guidance. *"You need to help her."* Walking over to the rock where Nan was massaging Rachel, Raven tried one last time for an out.

"So, Nan, are you a massage therapist or something?"

"No... I'm just trying to help Rachel..." Nan's intention was so pure, so hopeful, so trusting.

Raven decided she had no other choice. She took a deep breath, closed her eyes, and prayed. Raven invited the Light, and asked for the assistance of everything holy in a million mile radius.

She called upon Jesus, the Archangels, Mother Mary, and anyone else of benevolent intent who wanted to join the party.

She was taking no chances. *"Please help me!* Please guide me!" Raven prayed fervently. Raven asked Rachel, "Would you mind if I gave it a go?"

Rachel was weary but hopeful. "What have I got to lose? I'm not going anywhere right now!"

Trembling with nervousness and struggling to take a deep breath herself, Raven kneeled down beside Rachel's hips and scanned her body with the palm of her hand for energy blocks. She closed her eyes to concentrate. The roar of Vernal Falls and her own inner Guidance was now all she heard.

Within moments, Raven saw in her mind a map of Rachel's body with bundles of blocked energy highlighted everywhere Raven needed to work. As she extended her hand to touch the first block near Rachel's hip, Raven felt a huge rush of light and love pour through her with more intensity than she had ever experienced before at a workshop or in her private meditations. It was as if Vernal Falls had converted from thundering water to pure white light and she was sitting directly under it.

Raven began reciting the Aramaic Lord's Prayer to herself as she worked to maintain a loving, focused, healing vibration and stay out of her head and grounded firmly in her heart. One by one, she sensed the blocked areas in Rachel's body.

Raven felt a warm prickly sensation against the palm of her hand as a clue for when she was on target.

She gently massaged each tense bundle, directing the healing light through the crown of her head and out through her heart chakra and into the palms of her hands. She felt the blocked area crumble underneath the skin and dissipate.

Raven went to each area, one after the other, until she had worked through everything she saw on the map in her mind and could no longer sense any blocked areas with her palm.

Raven had no idea how long the whole event took.

She had blocked out everything but the sound of the falls, her focus on the prayer and being a conduit for healing love for Ra-

Scene Fifteen: Vernal Falls

chel. When she had done all she was guided to do, Raven opened her eyes to see all of her camping buddies standing around them with expressions of awe and amazement.

Raven gently and tenderly helped Rachel sit up. As she balanced herself, Rachel looked groggily at Nan and said, "What just happened?"

"Well, from over here it looked like God just gave you a massage and used Raven to do it!"

Then, to everyone's amazement, Rachel stood up and walked fluidly as if absolutely nothing had ever happened to her! Rachel smiled and thanked Raven. "I don't know what that was... but thank you. I can't remember when I've ever felt like this before."

The women sighed with relief and hugged Rachel as they walked over to the railing near the falls to take a group picture. Nan stayed behind with Raven at the rock as the others went to take pictures.

"I felt something wash over me right when you touched her." she said, her eyes wide. "It was powerful. There was so much love, this incredible energy... and you were *glowing*! I'm serious. There was this huge white radiant glow all around you! I could actually *see* it."

Raven hugged Nan and thanked her for giving her the nudge she needed in order to trust her own Guidance. She wondered what would have happened that afternoon if Nan hadn't taken Rachel over to the rock and started working on her. Raven realized that the power, the Guidance, and the ability all showed up just one second after she reached out her hand and took an action on faith.

She had asked for help to do the impossible, she was willing, and she took the leap even when she feared it would make her look like a total nut job to all her friends.

At the same time, Raven had to acknowledge that she had been preparing for that moment for five years.

She had spent two years memorizing the Aramaic Lord's prayer, had done dozens of intuitive bodywork sessions at workshops, and most importantly had learned to discern the voice of Guidance and trust it. This whole situation proved to her that miracles could happen when preparedness aligned with complete trust.

Looking back on the The Vernal Falls Incident, Raven couldn't help but see the connection to her work with the Master Key. She had spent a lifetime preparing for something she never could have expected. Guidance gave her exactly what she needed, exactly when she needed it, and no more.

Raven realized she was always on a "need to know basis," and she was grateful sometimes that her task had been revealed gradually. If she had known everything ahead of time, she never would have believed any of it. She would have thought herself grandiose or in need of a mental facility.

Raven returned to the present moment as a young bearded man wearing a knit beanie, T-shirt, shorts, hiking shoes and a kitchen apron delivered her breakfast.

"We've just about finished packing that trail sack lunch you ordered." he said. "You can pick it up on your way out."

Finishing her breakfast some twenty minutes later, Raven visited the spa below the cafe to make a reservation for a steaming hot essential oil bath after her hike.

Raven loved the fact that an elegant full-featured spa with hot tub, steam rooms, massage therapists, a yoga studio, and private baths was tucked away below this rustic time warp cafe from the mid-seventies. The money she saved on lodging, she gladly spent on spa services.

"Why spend a lot of money on a place you're in for just a few hours completely unconscious?" she reasoned. It was not terribly surprising she would appreciate something that was not what it seemed on the surface. "Takes one to know one." she thought.

Scene Sixteen

The First Gift

Ninety minutes away from the breakfast table, Raven had prepared her day pack, driven to the park, and arrived by park shuttle to the trail head for the Mist Trail and Vernal Falls.

She had hiked this trail at least four times prior to today, so she knew what to expect. At least, she knew what to pack and how to pace herself. Since she began working with the Master Key, Raven no longer pretended to know what to expect otherwise.

All her meditations leading up to this hike showed her reaching the falls and spending several hours meditating there. Half Dome was known to be a powerful energy vortex among people who were discerning of such things, and Raven had always noticed that she felt very peaceful and grounded whenever she was there.

Raven paused at the beginning of the trail head where a sign detailed the number of miles and kilometers to various points along the trail. She adjusted the straps on her day pack for comfort, tested the valve for her hydration system through a tube that emerged from her pack, and checked her boot laces.

Raven grasped her tall hiking stick lightly. Her hand-crafted staff was a gift to her from Nan after their experience at Vernal Falls two years ago. Nan's husband carved and polished walking sticks, and this one stood as high as her ear lobe and featured a woven leather strap decorated with colorful beads.

She found it especially useful in the steep jagged terrain on the second leg of the hike after the foot bridge, and it was comforting to steady herself on the descent.

Raven was always surprised by the number of total strangers who would pass by in either direction and admire her walking stick and say something to her or want to know if she got it in the gift shop. There was something very commanding about it, certainly.

It was "old school" with a craftsman's attention to detail unlike the fancy metal high-tech ones many hikers carried. It was also finished and polished and obviously not a random stick she had picked up on the trail. The leather strap and beads swung forward and back like a pendulum with every step.

As she started up the paved pathway, Raven made a point of connecting with the energy of the earth through the soles of her feet. She invited the Light in the form of the Father Energy through her crown chakra, seeking guidance. Then she breathed in the aspect of Light she had come to recognize as Child energy through her feet.

Child energy was about listening, accepting, and trusting in Divine Guidance. It was all about walking one's path and being willing to embody love on the Earth.

Raven could not think of a more appropriate walking meditation. As she took each step, she chanted silently in her thoughts the part of the Aramaic Lord's Prayer that helped her attune to Child energy, "TeyTey Malkutakh. "With every step she affirmed the divine "I can" of the cosmos, and her willingness to step forward in trust.

This hike was much less eventful than her journey two years ago. Raven stopped periodically to enjoy the view, take a picture, watch the birds, or enjoy a water or snack break. Even as she reached the final climb to the falls, she noticed that the Mist Trail was much less misty in October than it had been back in May 2008.

The weather was cool and the park sparsely populated. Raven remembered that it was not only a Sunday afternoon but that families with children had been back in school since September.

Scene Sixteen: The First Gift

This was a perfect day to run a divine errand.

Within ninety minutes, Raven reached the summit of Vernal Falls and found a place to sit down and enjoy the lunch packed for her by the Cafe. She noted the rock where she had worked on Rachel and spent a few moments basking in the memory of that day, seeing the events unfold like ghosts of her past in another dimension.

A family was having a picnic lunch on the rock where it all happened. She wondered if they could possibly have any idea what had happened there.

Raven unexpectedly tapped into other scenes from this place as well. Some were tragic and filled with despair as friends and families had lost loved ones to the unrelenting and powerful undertow of the falls. Most scenes she accessed were peaceful and reflective as hikers simply enjoyed the view.

"If these trees and stones could talk." she wondered. "I bet they would have some amazing stories to tell." What she didn't realize at the moment was that the trees and stones were "talking" just now, and she was seeing in her mind by clairvoyance what they had to communicate.

After eating her lunch, Raven picked up her pack and moved to a more secluded and private area away from the falls. She kicked off her hiking boots and set up a small comfortable blanket and sat down on a patch of earth between the boulders to meditate.

Breathing in, she invited the Light to guide her. She followed the breath as it filled her lungs from the bottom up and expanded her abdomen. Soon she felt one with the earth against her bare feet, the sounds of the rushing water, the chirping song of the birds.

Raven visualized a beam of golden light extending from her tailbone down through the granite, down through the crust of the Earth, down through the magma all the way to the very iron core center of the Earth. She imagined this beam of light anchoring to the Earth's core and creating a foundation from which a very strong cable as wide as her hips attached her to the Earth's center.

Raven felt completely one with All That Is. She felt peaceful, light, full of joy, and fully present. After enjoying this state for some time, Raven imagined the symbol she had intuited and designed forming in the center of her chest in her heart chakra.

The Master Key symbol was ablaze with white and golden light that permeated its center and emanated out through the rays and nodes of its geometric structure. She watched in her mind's eye as it slowly grew, and spun slowly on its axis like a view of the Earth from space.

Soon, the Master Key sphere grew to encompass her body, then encompassed her energetic field in about a ten- foot radius, then it gradually grew larger and larger until it embraced the entire mountain.

Raven visualized the center core of the symbol extending thousands of feet above and below her, permeating the Earth and the atmosphere. She allowed herself to breathe into it all of the love, healing power, and intentionality towards Oneness she cold imagine.

"I gift the Master Key to the Earth, to this sacred place, and to all that desire to connect with the love, healing and oneness it represents." she prayed.

Raven asked for the support of the Divine and all Divine beings. She asked for help to ground the symbol within her body and within the Earth. She asked for guidance and understanding to know what to do and when to do it. Finally, she expressed gratitude for the people and circumstances that had brought her this far.

When there seemed to be nothing else to do or say, Raven slowly brought her awareness back to her physical reality. She visualized the Master Key sinking into the ground and being absorbed by it in the way parched ground laps up the first summer rain.

When she opened her eyes, Raven saw the same trees, granite boulders, and pine cones. She watched the same squirrels climbing up and down the trees with morsels in their mouths stolen from hiker's lunches.

Only the scene was not at all the same.

Everything was... more saturated, more *vibrant*. The sounds of the waterfall and the wind in the trees were more clear and seemed to flow through her and within her being.

The visual world reminded her of getting her first pair of prescription glasses and seeing the world more vividly than she could ever remember—but it was more.

Raven felt as if she could sense the living energy of the natural world and that she could communicate with any part of it.

The world around her no longer felt... separate.

The feeling made Raven laugh out loud like a child on the beach, giddy with the sensation of sand between her toes. Raven could not remember the last time she felt so completely alive.

"So, this is what grounded really means!" she thought.

Raven was reminded of a verse from the prayer, "...thy kingdom come... on Earth, as it is in Heaven..." What if she was, in fact, experiencing that fusion of heaven and earth—that integration of Divine life energy from within the dense physicality of matter?

Suddenly the term "Divine Child" actually had meaning.

She felt as though the Divine was experiencing this physical place and time from within her very being, and she was completely and simultaneously conscious of the Divine in all, above all, and through all.

"*I pray that you would be in me and I would be in you and we would be one with the Father.*" were the words John had recorded from The Master.

"And so it is..." Raven smiled as she took in the view of the majestic valley stretched out below her. "This is *that* Oneness."

With that, Raven packed up her gear and put her hiking boots back on her feet to hike back down the mountain. She wondered if the hot private bath she had scheduled at the spa would be even better with this new level of awareness.

It was an enticing theory to test, anyway.

Scene Seventeen

Temptation

A hot steaming bathtub awaited Raven at the spa when she arrived. Ushered into a private room with elegant tile floors, Raven stroked her hand across the thick white towels folded for her use on a small chair.

Nearby was a cozy plush terry cloth bathrobe draped over the back of the chair for changing. Against the wall was a claw-foot jet tub releasing the fragrances of lavender and chamomile essential oils. Soft music played in the background from a CD player on a cabinet that was lined with softly glowing candles.

Raven felt like royalty. She reminded herself that "self-care" needed to move up a few notches on her list of priorities. She undressed and eased her tired and aching body into the hot steaming bath.

No matter her level of fitness, climbing a rocky, winding set of stairs in heavy hiking boots for four hours had extracted a fair toll on her energy reserves.

"Aaaaaaaaaaagggggghhhhhhhhhh..." her sigh lifted up toward the ceiling along with the scented wisps of steam.

Reflecting on her day, Raven was still in awe of the peace and the connection she felt with All That Is. She could not imagine a more perfect, more wonderful day.

Sitting in the bath, just breathing, Raven began to think

about the things Susan had said in her consultation. She thought about the magnitude and the importance of her task. She wondered why she, of all people, had been given this particular life purpose.

Raven thought about her experience on the mountaintop, and how she had brought the symbol holographically right out of her heart chakra and been able to expand it with her imagination and intention.

Losing herself to the memory, Raven was soon playing with the energy of the Master Key in the bathtub. She imagined it floating out from her heart and spinning in front of her. Raven extended her hands in front of her and began to spin the ball of energy faster and faster and expand it and contract it at will. She realized that her qi gong and tai chi practice had improved her awareness and sensitivity to energy in ways she did not expect.

Like a skilled apprentice of the Harlem Globetrotters, she expertly manipulated the ball of energy— spinning it, twirling it on a single finger, and performing tricks of grace and dexterity. Raven played giddily with the ball of energy.

The feeling was intoxicating.

"Brilliant." she thought, catching herself. "Here I am embodying a sacred symbol that has the power to possibly raise the consciousness of the planet and I have turned it into my own personal bath toy. What am I? Three?"

Raven had already crossed the line however. She was feeling a surge of power, a sense of hubris that came from being able to manipulate the ball of energy at will.

Like a child chasing the dog with a 4th of July sparkler, she recklessly pursued this expanding feeling of euphoria. It was *addictive,* and she felt incredibly special. Raven spun the energy ball faster and faster until suddenly the music on the CD player inexplicably cut out in the middle of a song and stopped completely.

The sudden silence halted Raven's play and she recognized the same warning signs in her body she had experienced in Madame Zelda's consultation parlor.

She was feeling a hyper, "sugared-up" feeling combined with a sensation like fish hooks digging in to her scalp and a weight

Scene Seventeen: Temptation

the size of a grapefruit in her stomach.

"Oh, crap!" she exclaimed in the direction of the bathrobe lying on the chair. Raven immediately stopped playing with the ball of energy, and put her damp, wrinkled finger tips over her face.

"Oh... I am *so sorry*. Please forgive me..." she said to no one in particular but the Universe in general.

Raven suddenly realized that this had been a test. Perhaps one of her own making, but still a test. She wasn't exactly sure if she had passed it.

The energy she was playing with and the Master Key were not the problem. Even the joy of her play was not the problem.

Her own Ego smuggled in a single seed of a thought, the idea of *specialness*, and made the Key and her connection to it mean something it was never intended to mean.

The Master Key was all about Oneness, Healing, and Love. Her Ego was crying out, "Look at me! I'm special! I'm different! I'm *better than!*" The two beliefs were obviously opposed to one another. Raven slumped down into her tub with a sigh.

She asked of Guidance "How can I fix this? Maybe this whole crazy project should be given to another! I'm not worthy... do you really think you can trust me with this? Look what I just did!"

Raven created a space in her heart to hear the answer. Clairaudiently, the voice of Guidance was clear and direct,

"Feeling 'less than' isn't the right answer either. This was merely a temptation. No harm done. You have learned to recognize the vibration and the feeling in your body when illusion and deception are within you. You experienced the temptation and then made a different choice. That is enough. You have chosen love and chosen not to be 'better than'. Remember that you are always unique, so there is no need to be special. Now forgive yourself and choose to not be 'less than' either. Tomorrow you will better understand this lesson."

Raven breathed in deeply as she felt a wave of peace return to her. A vision materialized inwardly of her sitting by a stream at the foot of a large stone monument on the valley floor—she thought she recognized it as Cathedral Rock. She determined that would be the focus of her visit to the park for tomorrow.

The water in the tub was now cooling off as was her desire to be anything more than a simple channel for the Divine.

Raven dried off and put on a clean set of sweats and an over-sized T-shirt. Walking out of the spa and into the cool of the night she began her ascent up the plank steps to CHIL-D.

Pausing at the metal railing at the top of the steps, Raven looked up into the vast starry sky. Amazed at how many stars she could see here, Raven felt as if she could see all the way into the center of the Milky Way Galaxy. Just then, she saw a shooting star directly overhead. She chose to interpret it as a sign—a nod of encouragement from the Universe.

"Thanks." She conversed with the heavens, "I needed that."

Scene Eighteen

Cathedral Rock

The slower pace and uncrowded space of Monday in Yosemite supported Raven's intention for the day. She drove through the valley with her sun roof open and parked near Cathedral Rock.

Sitting for a moment in the car, Raven breathed in the fresh autumn air laced with earthy pine. Directly in front of her gaze, three large ravens descended and perched on the fence by the trail head. Raven climbed out of the car to get her pack and a blanket from the trunk.

The ravens remained at their post.

"CAW! Caw, Caaaw!" one of the ravens shouted in greeting.

Raven Tahara giggled. "Well, good morning gentlemen! It seems I have the right place!"

The spokes-raven for the group dismounted from the fence post in a single hop and began to dance around on the ground just feet from where Raven stood.

"CAW!" his feathers bristled around his neck as he performed his ritual dance in the parking lot.

"Yes, my friend, I hear you. I understand. And thank you for the enthusiastic welcome!"

Raven was glad to be here alone. She might hesitate to hold

conversations with animals if she had come with friends. None of this seemed odd to her any more.

The entire world was open, and she felt connected to every animal, tree, wildflower, and blade of grass. Why wouldn't she be able to communicate with both the natural and supernatural world? They were all communicating perfectly to her.

A breeze rustled the pine boughs above her as Raven hiked through a short tree-lined pathway to a clearing by a stream. A man in his early sixties wearing waders cast his fly reel downstream while his female companion relaxed in a lawn chair with her book.

Animated voices echoed out of the forest as a large family gathered for what seemed like a family reunion. As car doors opened and shut, children laughed and chased one another while adults hugged and chatted about common things like clothes "oh, that looks darling!" and hotel coffee "tastes like sewer water!" and uncommon things like bear sightings "they were so cute! I got a picture—see!"

Raven could feel their connection, their love for one another, their joy in being together. It wasn't just the animals and plants she noticed, but every living thing.

She noticed the subtle difference between the human interactions and presences and those of the animals and the trees. The human world felt out of sync with the natural rhythms of nature like a one-man band on a unicycle tearing across the stage during a performance of Swan Lake. Even still, there was love in their voices and it passed between them much as the food passed around their picnic tables—freely shared and enjoyed.

Raven hiked about a quarter mile up stream until she found a sandy stream bed where she could sit quietly for the day. The first item out of her bag was her leather bound journal and a netted zipper pouch full of artist's markers. She laid them aside on her pack on the ground as she spread out her blanket and chair and prepared for today's lesson.

Settling in with a deep breath for meditation, Raven decided to focus on the aspect of the Light she recognized as the Mother energy today. While Father energy was helpful for vision and direction, and Child energy helped her connect to walking her path as a Divine

Scene Eighteen: Cathedral Rock

Child, Mother was the energy she sought to nurture and develop her creation. Like a vast nurturing womb, the Yosemite Valley powerfully cradled and supported her.

Raven invited the Father energy through her crown chakra, the Child energy through her feet, and then focused her awareness on her second chakra a short distance below her belly button. The energy of Mother was soft and formed a sphere of Light in her abdomen.

She meditated on the second verse of the Aramaic Lord's Prayer, "Nethqadash Schmakh." The prayer in its original wording was about creating sacred and healing space and connecting all the myriad facets of creation one to another.

As she breathed into her core, the sphere of Light expanded until it encompassed her, then grew to about six feet beyond her physical body. She sat with the energy for a time, and then invited this feminine aspect of the Light to guide her today. Feeling complete and ready to listen, she opened her eyes.

The steep granite wall of Cathedral Rock rose up as high as a fifty story building from across the stream in front of her.

Raven opened her journal and picked up a pencil and a medium grey marker and began to sketch. She knew that one of the best ways for her to be fully present to Guidance in the moment and simultaneously see deeply into what was around her was to draw.

Within moments her mind was quiet, and her fingers were busy capturing the edges and the shapes of the rock formation, the nearby trees, and the gnarled wind-carved pines that grew high above out of the monument's craggy outcroppings.

She drew the flowing stream, the brown speckled female mallard that cut through the water's glassy surface, and the leaves that fluttered and fell into the water whenever a breeze wafted through the valley floor.

Most interesting in this scene was an aspen tree that had fallen out over the water, creating an arch that suspended the trunk and boughs just a few inches from the water's edge. The base of the tree and root structure had become so loose from being saturated by water that a strong wind had blown it over.

Raven noticed a strange feeling of resentment toward the

tree for "ruining" her picture. If she drew such a scene for a painting in a gallery, she would never think to capture it like this.

Everything else was so picturesque and post-card-perfect and then here was this messy tree falling over right in the middle of it. The roots were exposed and covered with thick damp mud. The trunk projected out over the water at an awkward angle.

But the exercise was not about creating a perfect picture. She was here to really see and learn and experience what was around her. Raven was determined to be present to her experience, and drew precisely what was in front of her, accepting it and loving it with her eyes and her awareness.

In that moment something surprised her.

She felt a wave of loving compassion and knowing come over her. Suddenly, she saw the tree and its place in the picture as stunningly beautiful. It was, in fact, the most alive and interesting aspect of the entire scene!

The drama, the strength, the hidden backstory—all of it materialized in her imagination.

Raven watched as she visualized the scene that may have brought the tree to this moment. She sensed the tension between the root structure clinging to the soggy soil on the river embankment and the pull of gravity drawing it closer to the water's edge.

The tree was fighting for its place in the world as a living organism. Clinging to the soft embankment, it was somehow holding fast yet calmly surrendered to its inevitable fate. By this time next year, the weight of snow would certainly push its trunk under the water's surface and it would become a hiding place for fish and ducks.

As Raven filled in the scene with the twisted muddy roots springing from the stream bed, she felt a reverence for this tree. She was determined to capture it as the heroic figure she suddenly recognized it to be. When her sketch was complete, Raven sat and just observed the scene around her, following every detail and edge with her eyes.

School was now in session. The same voice Raven knew as Guidance arose from within her thoughts,

"You see the huge rock reaching up proudly into the sky? You

Scene Eighteen: Cathedral Rock

identify with it, don't you?"

Raven admitted that she did. The same part of her that experienced a specialness spasm in the bath last night, her Ego, was very eager to see herself as the Most Valuable Player in the scene.

"And how would this place feel to you if everything but the massive rock formation were gone? What if it was just a big rock in the middle of an asphalt parking lot in Bakersfield?"

Raven was amused when Guidance softened a sharp point with a little humor.

She imagined the scene without the stream, the trees, the aspen suspended over the water, the mallard swimming past. What if the little tufts of grass and wildflowers were gone? Would photographers from all over the world still find this tower of granite so beautiful?

What about the *community* of stone monuments that made up this amazing valley—Half Dome, The Three Brothers, El Capitan, and the breath-taking waterfalls? Would Cathedral Rock be anywhere near as stunning by itself?

No. It was the whole symphony—the harmony and variety of colors, textures, scents, and energies that made this the astounding place what it was.

Raven understood. No matter the significance of her task, she was only part of a bigger picture. Everything did not depend on her, but she could gratefully choose to play her part in harmony with all the other parts being played at this time.

"Your assignment for the rest of your visit is simple," Guidance continued, *"wherever you go throughout your travels today, whenever you encounter another human being, say to yourself these words, 'No Greater. No Less. All One Love'. Within every set of eyes, look for the Divine spark within each soul. You are looking at God through those windows and God is looking back at you. Every expression is a Divine expression. If you can see the beauty and strength and courage of this aspen tree, you can see the beauty in every person you meet."*

Raven agreed to practice. She pulled out her journal and wrote down what she had just intuited, how she felt, and what she had learned. She was curious how this exercise would play out over the next day and a half.

As she felt her stomach gurgle, she knew an opportunity to practice was coming soon. Time for lunch. Time to find a place to eat filled with bustling crowds and lots of human faces.

"No Greater. No Less. All One Love." she reminded herself.

Scene Nineteen

Dancing in the Street

"If you're going to ground, learn from the trees." Raven thought to herself. Driving up Highway 41, she decided to seek out lunch and visit the biggest trees in the valley, the residents of Mariposa Grove.

The route took her through a serpentine, tree-lined path where sunlight streamed through the pines and redwoods and cast dappled shadows on the freshly paved asphalt.

Raven was delighted to have such a smooth and tranquil drive, feeling fortunate to visit the park just as a huge road construction project was finishing up.

Enjoying a casual pace, she often pulled over to let other drivers pass. As each hurried driver flew past, Raven made a point to make eye contact from within her rear view mirror and practice her lesson for the day, "No greater. No less. All one love." she reminded herself.

She found today's practice took the edge off the annoyance she would normally feel in this situation.

Twenty minutes from the south entrance, the traffic halted.

Raven could see over fifty cars backed up ahead of her. The traffic moved only slightly faster than the glaciers that had once formed this valley.

Irate travelers periodically pulled out and turned around,

impatient with the standstill.

After twenty-five minutes of creeping along at two miles per hour and burning up nearly the last gallon of her $4.89 per gallon gas, Raven decided to pull into the last and only station she would see within thirty miles of the park.

The station and the Quik Mart were her only chance to re-fuel her car and her belly for the rest of the afternoon.

"Better take it." she thought. In the time it took to fill up, something very strange had happened. Raven looked out towards Highway 41 and was stunned to see not a single car on the road.

Standing in the middle of the road was a solitary construction worker wearing a sun hat and holding a reversible sign that said alternately, "STOP" or "SLOW." The worker holding the sign was a petite brunette woman perhaps in her forties wearing jeans, a white T-shirt under her bright orange reflective vest, and a pair of work boots.

She looked weary.

Raven wondered how long she had been directing traffic through the construction zone, and how many grumpy people she had encountered already.

Still practicing, Raven said to herself, "No greater. No less. All one love." as she made eye contact with the sign holder.

"Can I turn left to go south?" Raven inquired.

"Not yet." the worker replied. "There's another flag person two miles down the road who is waiting for the traffic I just sent through to clear. When I hear from him, I can let traffic from this end by."

"Oh." Raven replied. "So about how long, do you guess?"

"Could be another five to ten minutes." she replied.

Raven shut off the engine and put the car in "park."

Raven realized this was the most she had conversed with another human being in two days. So far, Raven's visit to Yosemite had been a solitary and reflective one. She had no idea how much her energy had shifted until she experienced what came next.

"Yeah, it's a tough job..." the flag worker started in. "Sometimes I'm on my feet for six to eight hours at a stretch. Yesterday I didn't get a single break because we were short two people..."

Scene Nineteen: Dancing in the Street

Raven just nodded and said, "Really?"

"Oh yeah. And the worst part was I had the most painful case of diarrhea I have ever experienced! Can you imagine? Here I am crossing my legs and clenching my cheeks and doing everything I can to not lose it!"

The flag worker began to rock back and forth between her toes and heels and slide from side to side with her legs together demonstrating her "diarrhea dance" for Raven.

"I'm calling in on the radio trying to get some *relief* (and I mean that in every sense of the word!) and I can't tell anyone my personal business because it would be unprofessional, you know. But I'm just dying out here! I mean, I was starting to *sweat!* Finally, the lady that works at the store here agreed to hold my sign for a couple minutes so I could use the toilet. Thank God for her! Oh, but if my boss found out about that I'd get fired for sure. But that's what they get for not sending anybody to help. That's what I figure."

"Wow," was all Raven could come up with. She was stunned at the extreme level of openness and comfort with which this total stranger shared things she would certainly regret later.

Then Raven remembered that she had spent all morning meditating and embodying the vibration of Mother energy. She was transmitting a feeling of nurturing, comfort, and support. Not only that, but her energy was magnified and enhanced not only by the powerful energy of Yosemite but also the Master Key. This hapless stranger was soaking in loving acceptance! Yesterday's diarrhea of the intestines had become today's diarrhea of the mouth.

"This poor woman," thought Raven. "She is going to wonder for days what came over her to share all of this with a total stranger in the middle of Highway 41."

Just then, the worker's walkie-talkie beeped and a voice from the other end of traffic announced. "All clear!"

Raven smiled. "*Yes. Yes it is.*" she thought.

The worker flipped her sign around from STOP to SLOW and waved Raven out onto the highway.

"Nice chatting with you! Have a nice day!" she smiled and waved with her free hand.

Raven waved back. "Hang in there! Hope today goes better for you!"

As Raven traveled down the highway, she was reminded of how much one person's state of mind could affect others — without ever saying a word.

The connection she felt with the Divine and with nature had now become evident in the people around her as well. The construction worker simply mirrored back her own increasing openness, authenticity, and emotional availability.

Scene Twenty

The General

Within minutes, Raven had reached the parking lot for Mariposa Grove, home to over 600 giant sequoias. The most famous tree in the grove was estimated to be over 2,700 years old — the 224 foot high Grizzly Giant.

The route she chose would take her through most of the grove then end up at Grizzly Giant for the grand finalé. Raven collected her pack and walking stick and set out to hike the Outer Rim Trail.

As she hiked along, people speaking a variety of languages nodded and smiled or said, "Hello!" or "Good afternoon!" People stopped her for directions or with questions, or just began friendly conversations. The entire world felt open, friendly, accessible — one.

As she hiked, Raven noticed the vividness of the ferns and wildflowers. Enriched by the unmistakable scent of redwood, the earth was a dark reddish brown. She felt as though every one of her senses was magnified here.

One of the senses now seeking her attention was her sense of touch. Within her hiking boot, a small pebble had worked its way into an annoying spot right under her heel.

Raven leaned up against a stately redwood along the path to balance herself as she wiggled the pebble out of her shoe.

Touching the rough bark of the tree, Raven felt moved to bless the tree and thank it for supporting her.

With her thoughts and loving energy emanating from her hand, she simply said, "Thank you."

To her amazement, she heard a distinct voice arise from within her thoughts, *"You are welcome."*

"Am I now communicating telepathically with trees?" Raven wondered.

"You are not the first." she heard the same tree voice within her thoughts, *"We've been expecting you all day. The General is looking forward to meeting you..."*

"The General?" Raven asked. "Who is the The General?"

"The people today call him Grizzly Giant. The First People had their own name. You will experience the great tree as The General—commanding, powerful, and wise." the tree continued.

Raven seemed to recall Bennu mentioning that she had conversations with trees. Raven was so open and connected now, nothing surprised her anymore.

"Would The General like to receive my gift?" Raven asked the sequoia.

"Oh, yes, very much. He has been waiting..." the tree actually seemed somewhat impatient for a living thing that was several hundred years old.

"Then I am looking forward to meeting The General as well. Thank you for telling me."

Raven smiled and excused herself so that she might continue her hike to see the other trees and most especially The General. Suddenly, the forest was alive with a subtle hushed tree conversation. Their veil of silence had been removed and Raven could hear them whispering from one to another, *"She is here... The Master Key is here... The General... so pleased to meet you..."*

Raven now understood how some people became "tree huggers." There was so much loving energy radiating out from the trees, she wanted to hug every single one of them.

Within an hour, Raven had hiked the perimeter of the Outer Rim and found herself within a hundred yards of The General. She

Scene Twenty: The General

felt the great tree long before she saw it. In her thoughts, a deep resonant voice emerged.

"*Welcome... I have been waiting. So good to meet you at last... I have been expecting you.*"

As Raven stepped out from behind a cluster of redwoods, the ancient sequoia came fully into view.

Raven gasped. A wave of emotion swept over her that tightened her throat and caused her to spontaneously tear up.

Awe, just pure awe, permeated her being. "Majesty" was the word the came to mind. The General was sublime— magnificent. More than his astounding 224 feet of height and 31 feet of width, The General exuded an energy that was the essence of grounded greatness.

Raven felt as though she had entered the chamber of a king and was being received as an honored guest.

"So good to meet you as well." Raven replied, still amazed she was conversing with trees.

"There is something I have for you, and I am hoping you may have some wisdom to offer me as well."

Raven found a place to sit where she could meditate near The General. She set down her pack, pulled out her small blanket, and sat looking up at the enormous branches the size of a small bus.

Imagining all of the human history that had passed while The General grew from a seed the size of her open hand to what now stood before her, Raven continued to be inspired.

Raven removed her boots and socks and let her bare feet touch the soil. She breathed deeply and imagined her tailbone extending deep into the earth, intermingling with the root systems of the ancient trees. She felt a sigh from the trees as they welcomed the connection.

Breathing into her heart chakra, Raven imagined the Master Key symbol floating out like a bubble. It was as if she was breathing it out from her chest. The glowing, slowly rotating sphere grew to the size of the great tree and gently embraced it. What she envisioned was like a massive radiant snow dome with The General inside.

Raven sensed appreciative joy from the great sequoia.

Rousting her back from her otherworldly communion with the tree, Raven was interrupted by a crowd of picture-taking tourists just released from the captivity of their air-conditioned tour bus.

People lined up in groups of twos and threes and took pictures in front of the King of Mariposa Grove with as much reverence as they might afford a life-size cartoon character in an amusement park. There was much upward pointing and some "Ooooo" and some "Aaaaghhh" and a few people stopped for a time to really appreciate him.

Raven reminded herself to practice today's assignment and uttered to herself at least a dozen times, "No Greater. No Less. All One Love."

Within about ten minutes the tour driver called out to the crowd and they casually meandered back to their bus.

Raven felt like she had been enjoying a quiet conversation with a celebrity who had just been overtaken by a band of roving paparazzi.

The connection was still there.

"General..." Raven inquired, "What words of wisdom do you have for me? I have this Master Key symbol, but honestly I have no idea what I am supposed to do with it. I have been told to 'bring it forward' and gift it to the world. But how? When? I don't even really know **why**..."

"*You have been working on this project even longer than I have stood here, my dear. Lifetimes... so many lifetimes... Do you really believe there isn't some part of you that knows exactly what to do and when to do it? Your path with the Master Key is much like your journey through the grove today. You received the information you needed exactly when you needed it—not one minute sooner! When you arrived, your heart knew what you wanted to do. Your heart knew what you came for... to give your gift. You gave it freely to bless me, to bless the grove, to bless the entire valley.*

Our gift to you is the earth on which you stand. We are helping you ground and hold this energy so it can be magnified to bless the whole world. Your small human body could not possibly hold all of that power, Child. You must have strong roots before you can touch the sky!

Up until now, the Master Key has only been a seed within your energy field. As you planted that seed within the Earth and shared it with your Mother, she nurtured it and it grew. It will continue to grow in the months ahead. Your gift will grow to bless many."

Raven glanced down at the moldavite pendant hanging from around her neck. It was all there. The stone was a fusion of the celestial heavens with earth rock, all held by a loving human hand with vines growing upward to the sky. Bennu had seen it all intuitively.

"Well, of course," Raven was amused. "Bennu talks to trees."

Raven arose and collected her blanket and her pack. Before the next tour bus could stop, she thanked The General and offered him a deep respectful bow. He was, in fact, royalty.

"As are you, Child. As are you." she heard the deep majestic voice one last time as she journeyed onward down the path.

Section Three

Bringing it Home

Scene Twenty-One

The Best Defense

Raven awoke to the sensation of a wet kitty nose against her own. For a moment, she forgot she was back in her own bed, in her own apartment.

Grateful for the extra day she spent enjoying the spa services at the hostel, she was relaxed and feeling completely grounded.

"Okay, Isis. I know you missed me." Raven stroked the soft spotted fur of her Mau. Purring with contentment, Isis nuzzled in for some extra work on her ears. Isis approved of the new, more grounded Raven.

Raven rolled off her futon and started her morning routine. First, she moved through her qi gong exercises, then headed for the shower.

This morning she opted for tea instead of coffee.

"I'm feeling too good to get all wired up on caffeine right now." she remarked to Isis as she started the kettle to boil. Waiting for the kettle, Raven sat down at her kitchen table to sort through her mail from the past few days. Still lying on the table was the notice she had received from the Superior Court last week.

"Oh..." Raven felt a remnant of the weight in her stomach she experienced the day the letter had arrived.

To her amazement, the fear was not as great as she remembered. Still, there was an uneasy part of her that needed to look deeply into this. The weighty ball of anxiety in her stomach rose up with a flash of anger at its core.

"Oh, great." Raven looked at Isis as she finished her kibble. "Seems like you can always count on something to bring you back down to earth after a few days on the mountaintop."

Isis darted out on cue as the kettle wailed. Raven poured her tea and settled down into her red leather recliner.

"Let's get to the bottom of this." she thought. Breathing in, she invited the Father energy and felt the Light cascade through her body easily from head to toe.

"Nothing there." she noted. Nothing resisted the Light of guidance and direction from Father, so she ran a "diagnostic" with the next energy.

Breathing in again, she invited Child energy in through her feet. Child energy moved steadily up through her legs, through her knees, past her thighs and hips. This energy was about her walking her path, about being and embodying love while being fully herself.

Raven noticed the energy got stuck right in her belly. A little seemed to flow through, but it was as if a boulder had crashed into a stream.

"Right at the core of my self-esteem." she thought. "OK. What about this has to do with me not feeling worthy?"

Placing her hands on her stomach, Raven put her focus on the ball of anger writhing within her.

"What do you have to teach me?" she inquired of the boulder in her stomach.

Raven breathed into her belly and waited. Within a few minutes, she saw a movie in her mind of the client who was taking her to court. She remembered her last encounter with John The Client.

He had insisted on meeting after hours to accommodate his schedule. She complied.

He didn't sign her agreement because he was in such a hurry. She didn't insist.

He accepted her work at the time and took the artwork on a

Scene Twenty-One: The Best Defense

CD to use, then bugged her for weeks to make endless picky changes that far exceeded the scope of his project.

When Raven stopped giving her time for free to make him happy, John got angry and took her to Small Claims Court. The client thought that threatening her would persuade Raven to keep working just to please him. He was certain he would get what he wanted.

She had offered to make additional changes at her hourly rate, but he insisted that he was "not satisfied yet" and was entitled to her working until he was satisfied. Raven drew the line and suggested John find another designer.

"Here I finally stood up for myself and what does it get me?" she thought angrily.

Raven breathed even deeper into her belly.

"OK. So, what does this have to teach me? What is my lesson here?" she wondered.

"*No one can make you feel inferior without your consent.*" Guidance served up some classic Eleanor Roosevelt.

Raven looked more closely at the whole situation. What had been *her* part? What message had she given this client about how she deserved to be treated?

"I didn't honor a single boundary with this guy..." she realized. "I worked after hours, I didn't insist he sign my agreement, I let him keep badgering me for changes..."

"He felt he could do this because I didn't think I was worth treating any better! Then I grew a spine when I finally had enough, and so now he's testing my resolve..." At that moment a really radical idea jolted Raven.

"*Soul contract!*" Raven's eyes were wide open now.

"This guy is doing his job to push me into a corner so I learn to stand up for myself!"

Raven said aloud as she locked eyes with Isis from across the room. Isis winked at Raven as if to indicate she was on to something.

"Well, only one solution for that." Raven thought as she went back to her meditation.

Raven imagined John in her mind, standing in a peaceful garden. In the distance, a waterfall poured down into a tranquil stream that flowed through this place of safety in her mind. She invited the Light to help her see him clearly and better understand the situation.

Raven approached John from within the safety of her meditation.

"Thank you for the trouble you went through to show me how little I respect myself and my abilities. You had to spend a good chunk of time filing paperwork, preparing your case, and staying up at night rehearsing in your mind all the reasons why I am wrong and did such a terrible thing to you, huh?"

John scowled and folded his arms.

"You know, I can see that you are angry." Raven continued. "I bet you feel disrespected. I stopped returning your phone calls and ignored you. I bet you were afraid I was taking advantage of you..."

John seemed to be listening.

"How did it feel when I wouldn't give you what you wanted?"

"You were very unprofessional! The customer is *always* right! Haven't you ever heard that? The customer is *always right!*" John ranted.

"Even when the customer is taking advantage of another business owner?" Raven countered.

"I wasn't taking advantage! I'm *entitled*. I paid for this and I should get what I want. The customer is always right!" John repeated.

"The *customer* is always right, or *you* are always right?" Raven asked.

John looked like he had been slapped.

"Well, I *am* right about this! You'll see. We'll have our day in court and you'll see that the customer is always right."

Raven was amazed to see that as they talked, John seemed to slowly transform into a small boy about the age of three.

She recognized that the grown man who was suing her was in fact a very hurt and frustrated small boy who wasn't getting what he wanted. Raven intuited that he had been trained by other women, perhaps his mother, to always get whatever he wanted without regard to what was honoring the needs of both parties.

Raven found it much easier to have compassion for a three year old having a temper tantrum.

Scene Twenty-One: The Best Defense

"Hey there. Look… It's not so bad. I am not the mean lady you think I am. I just needed to learn an important lesson about saying "No" when someone drives a tractor right through my boundaries. I wasn't loving and respecting myself, see? You helped me to see that. You did a fantastic job and I am very grateful. You are a very clever boy."

The three year old Johnny brightened up.

"And something tells me that I promised *you* a lesson in return." Raven smiled at John the three year old. "Maybe you are going to get a lesson about being right, or about getting what you want."

"Oh, yes!" Johnny piped up. "I am most definitely going to get a lesson on being right! And I'm pretty sure I'll get what I deserve!"

"So, how about the soul that is Raven and the soul that is John The Client just say 'Thank you for the lesson' and we accept and respect one another for going to all this effort to help one another grow?" Raven suggested.

"You're not going to hug me or something sappy like that are you?" John folded his arms.

"Not if you don't want me to, but I am going to choose to love you." Raven chided. "You loved me enough to put me through all this just so that I would wake up and get some self-respect. I don't want to let either of us down."

Raven turned and left the three year old client in the garden. With a smile and wave one would expect from a calm parent, Raven simply added, "See you in court."

Scene Twenty-Two

A Good Offense

"*I would counter-sue his ass!*" Karly exclaimed with great indignation from across the coffee table at Old Soul. As if to mirror her internal state, the bean grinder from behind the service counter fired up with an angry growl. Raven, Karly and Bennu paused their conversation until the grinder was through with its untimely outburst.

"Are you *kidding* me?" Karly picked up where she left off. "Let me get this straight... You did over *five hours* of work for this guy, worked *after hours* to fit into *his schedule*, made several rounds of changes to make *him* happy after he had already accepted the artwork ... and he's suing *you*?

"*And* he ran a charge-back through the credit card company." Bennu jumped in. "So Raven was actually paid only half the money for all that work."

"And he's suing *you*?" Karly repeated exasperated.

Amazed that Karly was more upset over the court case than she was, Raven sighed deeply before responding to her protest.

"You know, I really spent some time looking into this. I happen to believe that situations like this come along to teach me lessons I've signed up for."

"You *can't* be serious." Karly interrupted.

"I *am* serious. The way I see it, John is here by appointment and he is doing his job perfectly. He has forced me to look at all the ways I sell myself short. I don't respect my own gifts and abilities, and I don't enforce boundaries with people who are not respectful of a balanced energy exchange." Raven said.

"Or *maybe*…" Bennu raised an inspired index finger, "John has some unconscious desire to be connected to you, to tap into your power and creativity. But you didn't give him what he wanted — that connection. You cut him off, so he's all confused and angry. In my opinion, he's just trying to force you to give him what he wants but he doesn't have the internal clarity or awareness to ask for it in an authentic way."

"You two are talking crazy talk." Karly huffed. "I would counter sue! I would *clean his clock*. I would show him who's boss! Can't you see he's trying to *get at you!* You're not going to *defend* yourself? What are you going to say in court?"

"I'm going to hold my space, trust divine guidance in the moment, and answer whatever questions the judge has with the truth as I perceive it. Just the facts, ma'm, just the facts." Raven's response was casual. Too casual for Karly.

"Don't you feel taken advantage of? Aren't you a *little* afraid? What if he *wins?*" Karly persisted.

Raven took a deep breath and a long swig of her Americano before taking another run at the padded wall that was Karly's position on the matter.

"Well, no… I don't feel taken advantage of because I believe that I set this up energetically with the opinions I have of myself. I am getting what I think I deserve. And yes, I am a bit nervous because, really, I just don't like conflict. I want everyone to *like* me. Obviously, that didn't happen here. But I thought about it and the worst thing that could happen is I would have to refund John less than $200 and I won't ever have to deal with him again. The court can't force me to work with him indefinitely to make him happy. So, I figure investing $200 to gain a major life lesson is a pretty reasonable fee for the seminar, you know?" Raven relaxed back into the coffee house sofa and rested her case.

Scene Twenty-Two: A Good Offense

"Well, I think that is ridiculous!" Karly insisted. "Obviously, you are right and he is wrong. You are a good person and he is a total jerk. If I were the judge, I would see that in a heartbeat and I would make him pay you!"

"It has nothing to do with being right or even being a good person, Karly." Bennu was almost as frustrated with Karly as Karly was frustrated with Raven. "The way things work in court is all about the *law*. The judge is going to find out what the contract between them was, and determine to what degree the contract was fulfilled and rule accordingly. This isn't some singing popularity contest on TV. No one gets to vote on who has the most goodness or likability. Frankly, I think Earth laws are so archaic. If people would just evolve and see one another as equals—if they would recognize that they are connected— there wouldn't be the need for these expensive little dramas."

"Not you too!" Karly protested. "You're not gonna go all high brow and spiritual with me on this."

Watching Karly sputter and fume, Raven finally caught on to what was *really* going on with Karly and why she was so upset. "Karly, why does this whole thing have you so upset? *I'm* the one going to court, not you." Raven inquired.

"Well, because I hate to see my friend (who did nothing wrong by the way) being treated like this. It's not fair! It's an outrage!"

The bean grinder roared again from behind the counter as Karly frowned and waited impatiently for it to stop. Raven and Bennu just looked knowingly at one another with sly half smiles. They both recognized the energy Karly put off was being reflected back in their environment.

"*Anyway...*" Karly's words tumbled into the space created by the now silent bean grinder. "As I was saying... it upsets me because it's wrong, and it's not fair, and I don't want someone taking advantage of you."

"You know, Karly, an idea I've been playing with for some time is that whenever something really upsets me, whenever something has a big charge to it, it's something for me to take a closer look at. Usually, when I think that someone else or some outer circumstance is the problem, what I'm most upset about is something within me. You're looking at my court case and taking it personally—as if you were the one going to court. You're acting defensive and angry as if you were the one on trial."

"Hey, you mess with my friend Raven, you mess with me!" Karly was resolute.

"While I appreciate the sentiment, would you be open to looking at this a little... deeper?" Raven asked.

"What do you mean?" Karly withdrew like a cockroach anticipating a light about to come on in the basement.

"Well... is there some part of you that feels taken advantage of or like you need to protect yourself?"

An awkward silence stood between them and Karly wished the bean grinder would start up again. No luck. Raven began to silently recite the Aramaic Lord's prayer in her mind to hold space for Karly. She knew she was standing on hallowed ground. Whatever happened in the next sixty seconds would be pivotal for Karly.

Karly's eyes started to well up with angry tears. Bennu shifted uncomfortably in her seat. Karly averted her gaze and began twisting the lid on her coffee in a slow, deliberate, and squeaky clockwise circle.

Her voice quivering with tears, Karly finally blurted out, "Oh, *come on*, Raven! You know what happened to me... you know what he *did*. I told you about that..." Karly bit her lip. The silence sat on her like a schoolyard bully. She did not want to continue. Not here. Not now.

Raven felt a growing ache in her heart as she empathically sensed Karly's old wounds. Raven continued to silently pray her prayer and hold space for Karly.

Finally, she just put her arm around Karly's shoulders and held her while she cried. Raven lost track of time as she focused all her heart and energy on Karly. She invited the Mother aspect of the Light to assist her and soon sensed a nurturing sphere of healing light had enveloped the two of them. It felt as though they were hidden from all the clamor of the coffee shop and stares of curious

Scene Twenty-Two: A Good Offense

onlookers. Raven held this space with Karly until she sensed her starting to shifting out of shock and despair.

"I'd rather go to court than have to feel this pain again!" Karly spat out the words as she sheepishly wiped snot off of Raven's shirt.

"So would I, Karly... So would I." Raven said with a hint of a smile. Karly surrendered into a surprised laugh. As she wiped mascara all over her fingers and started to resemble a raccoon, Karly recomposed herself.

"You were right all along, Raven. You told me this before. I need to look at this. I need to start the healing process. I just keep stuffing all this pain down inside, you know? I just don't want to have to feel it again... I'm afraid."

"I know." Raven whispered. "I've been there too. I spent over ten years peeling back the layers and shining the Light into every dark corner. But it gets better. You get better. And you come out on the other side stronger. It's kind of like when you break a bone and then it heals even stronger in the spot where you broke it. Hearts do that too, I think."

"I sure hope you're right." Karly sniffed.

"Hey, I'm going to court in two days and I'm not freaking out. That's something isn't it? Believe me, that's progress. I couldn't have done that five years ago. I sure couldn't have done that ten years ago. That's healing. That's transformation. It really can happen."

"Who wants chocolate?" Bennu chimed in.

"Me!" Raven and Karly responded in unison.

"Not if I get there first..." Bennu chuckled. "Geez, you two. This would never happen with three *guys* going for coffee!"

The three of them gathered their bags and made for the door. Raven wondered if perhaps in some serendipitous way her trip to court and today's discussion had been just the thing to get Karly started on her own healing journey. Regardless, Raven now had a greater appreciation for her own healing journey. In two days, she would know how much progress she had actually made.

Scene Twenty-Three

Judgment Day

"All rise!," the court bailiff announced as a room full of thirty-four anxious strangers stood in unison. The Bailiff was a tall, stocky, mustached man in his mid-forties. He wore a khaki olive green law enforcement uniform and sported a heavy leather belt with side-arm.

Raven was having difficulty imagining the circumstances in which he might use his shiny black revolver, but she had seen enough drama on *The People's Court* to accept that it was probably a good precaution.

"The Honorable Judge Johansen, Superior Court Judge for the State of California, Sacramento Small Claims Court, presiding." The bailiff announced the arrival of the judge.

The Judge entered from a side door at the front of the courtroom and tugged up the hem of his long black robe as he ascended three hidden steps behind the stenographer's post to his seat at the bench.

"You may be seated." Judge Johansen perfunctorily gestured to the group. As the Judge took his seat at the bench in a stately high back leather executive chair, Raven noticed for the first time something that made her giggle quietly. Soon, a broad smile emerged on her face. There behind the bench, like an enormous full moon, was the seal of the Superior Court of Sacramento. *Raven had designed the symbol for the court seal!*

The court had hired her eight years ago to create the design, and she had completely forgotten about it. This was the first time she had ever *been* in court. The only time she had ever seen it after the work was complete was when it showed up once a year on a postcard in her mailbox with a summons for jury duty.

The sight of her own creation completely dominating the "field of battle" was very comforting. Raven took a deep breath and looked at her watch as Judge Johansen instructed the plaintiffs and defendants on courtroom protocol and started up an orientation video.

"*Where is she?*" Raven looked at her watch again.

Raven knew she would need energetic support for her day in court. The environment was charged with anger, fear, judgment, betrayal, and pain. She knew it would be, and this was why she asked Sheryl to come and help her hold space during the proceedings.

Sheryl was Raven's "diving buddy." For the last seven years they had both been working diligently on their own inner growth and healing. They had attended many of Ania's workshops, and Sheryl knew how to work with Father, Mother, and Child energies. Raven knew two things for certain: Sheryl could hold the space for as long as it was needed without distraction, and Sheryl was always there or her.

If life could be thought of as a battle, Sheryl was the one in the fox hole next to her—the one who had her back. They had shed their share of tears, logged countless hours of emotional "processing" and seen each other through some of their toughest moments. They had always been blessed with the grace of not having both of them "go sideways" at the same time. It seemed that whenever one of them had something flaring up for attention, the other one was in a balanced place and able to help.

"At this time, The Court will take a twenty minute recess." Judge Johansen announced. "As you heard on the video, this is the time when plaintiffs and defendants will meet outside the court-

Scene Twenty-Three: Judgment Day

room to show one another any exhibits, evidence, or documents relevant to the case. Posted on the wall outside the door is the docket for today's proceedings. This will tell you the order in which you will be called to appear."

Judge Johansen seemed like a reasonable, intelligent man. With his distinguished salt-and-pepper, slightly thinning hairline and casual demeanor, Raven felt assured that he would be balanced and fair.

Stepping outside the courtroom's large wooden double doors, Raven immediately caught sight of Sheryl. She was standing just beyond another uniformed bailiff who was facilitating order amidst distracted pairs of plaintiffs and defendants.

Sheryl smiled and waved to get Raven's attention. Although she was just 5'6", she always seemed taller. Part of the effect came from her high heeled designer shoe collection and the rest was her growing energetic field.

Today she was dressed in business attire and had her long blonde locks pulled back into an all business ponytail with a clip.

"Hey there!" Sheryl greeted Raven with a hug. "Sorry I wasn't in there earlier. I got tied up with the security line going through the x-ray machine and they wouldn't let me in until now."

"No problem. I'm just glad you're here. Really glad. I need all the support I can get. It's icky in there."

"Lots of fear, I bet." Sheryl could already feel it herself. Raven sensed she was starting to kick into space holding mode already.

"Listen, I have to connect with John and do a little 'show and tell' exercise before the circus starts. How about you go inside and grab a seat while we get this out of the way?"

"Roger that!" Sheryl smiled and half pretended to salute like a soldier following orders into battle. Raven suspected there must be some past life between them where that may have actually been the case. The foxhole feeling was just so natural for them.

Raven turned around from talking to Sheryl to see John standing just four feet away. He was dressed in a freshly pressed business suit and tie and was leaning to one side slightly to accommodate a very large leather satchel hanging from a strap over his right shoulder. The two of them nodded at one another and walked without a word around the corner to a small table where they could show each other what they intended to present.

"Shall I go first?" John was very formal. Very curt.

"Oh sure. Go for it." Raven was somewhat flippant.

John opened his large leather satchel and pulled out a three-ring binder that was two inches thick. As he thumbed through the pages, she saw multiple copies of every e-mail they had exchanged over the course of their working relationship and the drawings Raven had produced at various stages of completion.

Missing, much to Raven's dismay was her standard agreement. John had been so pushy and the job had seemed so simple that she had not pushed him to authorize her standard agreement. Had she done so, this would never have come this far. The agreement had clearly stated what the project included and that refunds were not allowed for this type of work. It also stated that the client would seek mediation in the event of an issue rather than going right to court. It was too late for any of that now.

"So, what have you got?" John demanded.

Raven opened a slim leather folio that contained just three documents—her standard agreement, a sample of John's design as it was at the end of their process, and two pages of e-mails that detailed some final conversations between them as the relationship was imploding.

Raven noted that she had one page of dialogue in particular that John had not included. It was the e-mail where John had yammered on like a complete jerk and called her all kinds of names and threatened to sue her if he didn't get what he wanted when he wanted it. The e-mail also showed Raven's end of the conversation as being reasonable, professional, yet firm. She clearly did not look like someone trying to get away with something.

Still, Raven knew she didn't have a signed contract and two semesters of Business Law in college had left her with one inalienable fact, "Verbal agreements are as good as the paper they're written on." Not much.

For the first time since the whole ordeal started, Raven be-

Scene Twenty-Three: Judgment Day

gan feeling nervous as she took stock of John's substantial binder, multi-media visuals, and confident body language. John was clearly playing the psychological game as he snapped the satchel shut and offered Raven a rigid handshake,

"May the best person win." he smirked. He tilted his head to one side like a bird of prey considering its next meal.

"And may the truth come to light." Raven added. John sauntered back towards the open double doors to the courtroom and paused at the docket posted near the door. He glanced back at Raven looking smug. Every part of him oozed confidence and a sense of purposeful right-ness.

Raven felt a knot tighten in her gut. All of her meditations and preparations were suddenly feeling like a flimsy paper gown she would wear for a doctor's appointment—right down to the nagging feeling that her butt was exposed.

Scene Twenty-Four

Order in the Court

Raven found Sheryl seated in the courtroom with her eyes closed, clearly already on duty to help hold the space.

"Well guess what?" Raven interrupted Sheryl's zen-like state. "We're dead last on the docket. We're going to be here awhile."

"Nice." Sheryl responded dryly. "So how's Monkey Boy?"

Monkey Boy was Sheryl's nickname for John. The logo Raven had designed for his business, Champs, featured a chimp wearing a sports jersey with a big number one on it. The Champion Chimp had been John's bright idea and he redefined the term "anal" when it came to his perfectionism regarding the end product.

Raven savored the irony that here she was, being taken to court over not making a guy happy with his Champion Chimp logo, and the whole event was unfolding in the presence of a giant five-foot-in-diameter, metallic, gold-embossed seal of the Superior Court which she herself had designed.

"You just can't make this stuff up." Raven thought to herself.

Raven and Sheryl sat quietly as the court proceeded through its lengthy docket. Many of the cases were tenants and landlords in disputes about unpaid rent or damaged property. The most interesting case was a woman suing a man who had "damaged her boob job" by hitting her with his monster truck while she pumped gas at a crowded station. Apparently, he had impacted her in such a way that she could no longer make a living as a pole dancer at one of the local night clubs. She was "ruined" and could not imagine how she was going to feed herself without her most valuable assets.

Raven and Sheryl exchanged numerous amused glances throughout the Monster Truck vs. Boob Job case. It helped take the edge off the wait. Raven found it increasingly difficult to imagine, as each case was presented, that she might ever have some positive impact on transforming the consciousness of the planet. The world from this perspective was full of anger, fear, outright stupidity and an enormous need to be right. Every single person that stood before Judge Johansen was certain of one thing—they were *right*.

As the last two cases presented their arguments to the judge, Raven felt her stomach knot up again. Her mouth felt dry and her palms were beginning to sweat. She focused on her breathing and tried to relax—tried to somehow deepen it. Holding her own space was getting increasingly difficult. She was glad Sheryl had come.

"Hold Mother energy for me. I could sure use some nurturing protection." Raven looked nervous for the first time in weeks.

Sheryl placed her hand between Raven's shoulder blades and started running healing energy toward her heart. Within minutes, Raven started to feel calmer, more at peace.

Raven fidgeted with the closure on her leather folio and glanced at her three meager pages of "evidence." It was all like a bad flashback from her days on the high school debate team. She cringed at the memory of her debate partner forgetting and leaving all the evidence card boxes at home. Raven never liked debate. She never liked confrontation—period.

Glancing over at John seated four rows up to her right across the aisle, Raven noticed him flipping through his massive binder, writing little notes in the margins. He was checking some items on his laptop. He reminded Raven of a gladiator sharpening his sword before battle.

Raven focused on John and visualized white and gold light flowing down from above on to the top of his head, down through

Scene Twenty-Four: Order in the Court

his shoulders and into his heart. She imagined the light softening the parts that were hard and jagged, she imagined knots of anger and frustration untying. As she visualized the light compassionately working with John, she noticed a sensation of peace come over her. Raven remembered her meditation from last week about John. "He's just a frustrated three-year-old who didn't get what he wanted." she reminded herself.

"Will defendant Raven Tahara and plaintiff John Ratchette please approach the court?" the bailiff announced.

Raven gulped and felt Sheryl pat her shoulder as she stood up to approach the bench.

"I've got your back." Sheryl reminded her.

"Thanks." Raven glanced back over her shoulder. "See you on the other side."

Raven approached the podium on the left designated for the defendant. John took his position at the podium on the right and began unpacking his "ammunition."

Judge Johansen placed his reading glasses on the bridge of his nose and looked over a small stack of papers detailing the essence of their case.

As the judge thumbed through the stack of papers, John was rocking back and forth between his toes and heels, anxious to get in the fray. Raven thought he now looked like a boxer dancing in his corner, waiting for the bell to sound. Raven expected him to come out swinging.

Finally, the judge looked up from his papers, removed his glasses and addressed the two of them.

"It says here that the plaintiff, Mr. Ratchette, engaged the services of the defendant, Ms. Tahara, to create a logo for his business. The defendant is seeking restitution. He claims to have paid the defendant $495 for her services and not received the service for which he paid.

"I am going to give each party a few moments to tell me their side of the story and present any evidence they feel compelled to share with the court. I will ask you any questions I see as relevant to the case and then I will render my decision."

"Mr. Ratchette, you may proceed with your remarks."

John had apparently been waiting his whole life for this moment to play Perry Mason. This became evident the second he opened his mouth.

"Yes, Your Honor! I hired Ms. Tahara to create a logo based on a sketch I provided her with, detailed in Exhibit 'A'." John handed the paper to the bailiff who handed it to the judge. "My idea was a chimp to represent my business called Champs... it needed to have a sports jersey with a big number one on it."

The judge looked at the sketch through his half-lens glasses.

"But as you can see from 'Exhibit B', what I *got* was not an adequate representation of the concept!"

John handed another piece of paper to the bailiff who handed it to the judge. Judge Johansen studied Raven's work for about thirty seconds, then looked back up at John.

"Alright, Mr. Ratchette. It looks like a chimp wearing a sports jersey with a number one on it to me. How was this not in keeping with your agreement?" Judge Johansen inquired.

"Well, your Honor, when we created the original logo we spent quite a lot of time on it and I was very worn out by the end of the process. I didn't see at the time that Ms. Tahara had neglected to add the three dimensional shading I had requested to the chimp's back side."

Raven tried not to laugh out loud at the absurdity of being taken to court over the dark side of a monkey's butt. She bit her lip. She glanced up at the bailiff and the stenographer who seemed to be doing likewise. This case had excellent potential for eclipsing the Monster Truck vs. Boob Job case they had just witnessed on the grounds of pure comedic value. Still, the law is the law, and Raven knew she had no contract.

"Ms. Tahara, is it true that the plaintiff engaged you to create a logo for his business?"

"Yes, Your Honor."

"And how long have you been doing logo design?"

"About twenty years Your Honor."

"And when you engage a new client, do they typically sign

Scene Twenty-Four: Order in the Court

an agreement to work with you that specifies your working relationship and deliverables?"

"Yes, Your Honor. That is my standard practice. Unfortunately, in this particular case, I neglected to get a signed agreement from the plaintiff. I was meeting with him after normal business hours and I guess I wasn't as sharp as I would have been earlier in the day."

"Do you have a copy of your standard agreement?"

"Yes, Your Honor, I do."

Raven handed her agreement to the bailiff who passed it on to Judge Johansen.

"And what do you have to say about this shading issue on the chimp's back side?"

Raven thought she might guffaw any minute and blow her case completely. She could tell from a similar whimsical spark in the judge's eye that he was close to "losing it" as well.

"Well, Your Honor... I did make the effort. As you will see from this print-out, I adding shading to the chimp in the place specified... apparently it was not to the satisfaction of Mr. Ratchette. I created another version and e-mailed it to him with a slightly darker shadow, but he didn't care for that one either."

Raven handed the papers to the bailiff.

"Did you do anything to alter these logos since you presented them to the plaintiff? Did you change them in any way before appearing in my court today?"

"No, Your Honor, I have not changed these files since the day when communication broke down between us. What you are seeing now is exactly what he saw several months ago." Raven made a point of speaking directly to the judge and making consistent, heartfelt eye-contact. She knew he was an expert lie detector, and she consciously delivered her truth as effectively as possible.

"Mr. Ratchette, is there anything else you would care to share with this court?"

"Well, *yes*, Your Honor—I *do!*" John had now fired up his laptop and wanted to approach the bench. "Can I come up there? Can I show you this?"

"You may approach the bench." The judge conceded.

John hoisted his laptop awkwardly onto the judge's podium. "There! See that? See here?" John pointed feverishly at the screen. "There's no shading! This is the file she sent me. This came from the CD! Here's the proof!"

The judge summoned the bailiff to look at the screen.

"Do you see any shading on the monkey's behind?" he asked the bailiff.

"Well, I don't know... kinda."

"Show it to her." The judge gestured in the direction of the stenographer. The bailiff took the laptop over to the stenographer. She looked at the screen and shrugged.

"Could be. It's hard to tell. I think I see a little."

"Ms. Tahara, can you explain this discrepancy?"

"Yes, Your Honor. With graphics there are several variables that may account for a difference of perception in matters such as this. One factor is the quality of the computer monitor and another factor is the quality of paper used to print the image. Still another factor is the resolution of an image. High quality images have more data than lower quality ones. A web image at 72 dots per inch (dpi) will have less visual data than a print image at 300 dots per inch. The image I showed you earlier was a high resolution image printed on quality photo paper. These are the same variables I presented to the plaintiff when he accepted the artwork. I burned the CD, and he left that day with what I *thought* to be a finished project." Raven had slipped into geek mode but felt it was necessary under the circumstances.

"I see..." replied the judge.

"Your Honor?!" (John made the fatal mistake of addressing the judge without being asked.) "May I offer another perspective on this matter?"

"If you must." Judge Johansen raised a single eyebrow that told Raven he had just lost patience with John's Perry Mason routine.

"*Well*, Your Honor. You may not have direct experience with such matters as computers and graphics, so maybe I can explain it in another way..."

Raven was doing an inner cartwheel knowing he had just stepped in his own chimp poo. John was talking to the Superior

Scene Twenty-Four: Order in the Court

Court judge like he was a complete idiot.

"Imagine that I had hired Ms. Tahara to paint my house… and when I went out to inspect the job at the end of the day, because of way the light fell on it at the time, I *might* think everything was perfect. I pay her. She goes on her way. The next morning, the sunlight is hitting my house differently and I see that there is a spot missing I couldn't see the evening before. The job isn't done to my satisfaction! She should come back and do it right so that she meets the terms of our agreement, wouldn't you agree?"

John looked ridiculously pleased with himself. He beamed with his mastery of metaphor.

The judge looked at Raven with a sympathetic glance. One glance told her everything—John was toast.

"OK. I've made my decision!" The judge cleared his throat. "According to the judgment of this court, the plaintiff engaged the defendant to create a logo. The defendant created a logo and the plaintiff accepted the logo by taking delivery of the CD. *You owe her $495!*" Judge Johansen hammered his gavel down and just like that it was over. Raven had won.

John was caught completely by surprise.
"But! But! But…"

Raven turned on her heel and headed straight for the door. Sheryl was right at her back. As they reached the sunlit terrace outside the courtroom Raven and Sheryl exchanged a high five followed by a big hug.

"We *did it!* Oh, I am so relieved." Raven was gasping for her first deep breath all day.

Sheryl was chuckling as she thought back over the events of the last few minutes. She slid her sunglasses down to the end of her nose and then she did her best impression of the judge querying the bailiff and the stenographer, "Mr. Bailiff, do you see a shadow on this monkey's butt? How about you, Ms. Stenographer? Do you see a shadow on the monkey's butt?"

Raven was still partly in shock that the decision had come so quickly and so much in her favor. Still, she laughed.

The biggest source of fear in her life had just transformed into the biggest source of amusement. It was all made possible by surrendering the outcome and trusting in divine guidance and protection. She didn't have to present brilliant arguments or have a massive binder full of 'evidence.' Her accuser had demolished himself without any effort on her part. She had just embodied and lived out a concept she had recited hundreds of times, "*I surrender because I trust.*"

"And that, "she concluded "is probably one of the most important lessons of all."

As they made their way down the escalator to the parking lot, Raven turned to Sheryl and asked, "Have you ever heard the story about how ancient shamans could change the direction of a tornado?"

"No. What about it?" Sheryl asked.

"Well, they believed that the way you control a tornado is to understand it, to get inside it with your heart and see what the tornado needs. When you make what is outside *one* with what is inside, you can change what it does from within you."

"I hope this doesn't mean that now you're going to be a monkey butt!" Sheryl snorted as she laughed.

"You just like saying it, don't you?" Raven replied.

Their laughter echoed through the halls of justice as light streamed in through the tall glass windows. Bystanders looked confused as two middle-aged women descended the escalator exchanging a banter typical of two silly six-year-olds.

"Monkey butt! *giggle*

"Mon-key butt! " *snort.*

Scene Twenty-Five

Just Following Orders

Alex awoke to the jarring snarl of a chain saw outside his bedroom window.

"*Landscapers…*" he thought with a sigh. "Why do they have to start so early in this neighborhood?" The house he bought years ago was maintained by a maintenance crew paid for by association dues. Every Tuesday, the synchronized foliage assault team of mowers, weed-eaters, edgers, and pruning equipment was unleashed upon the neighborhood. Most of the residents were oblivious to their comings and goings, but Alex had a front row seat from his home office window.

Alex had been up half the night in worry over his planned brunch with Raven this morning. They had been on a "break" for several months to give their relationship some space, to sort out their feelings for one another, to try and figure out what to do next. The distance had been helpful for both of them. Like open wounds needing air to heal, the space they gave one another had at least brought them some perspective. They were each realizing that they certainly could live without the other, but now they were coming up against the big question, "Do I really want to?"

Alex reached for his smart phone and texted Raven to confirm. She texted back, "On my way."

Just as his feet touched the floor to head for the shower, the chain saw outside his window made a sound that was no longer the high pitched whine and buzz of pruning a few small limbs. It growled low as its metal teeth sank into something much more dense.

"NO!" Alex's eyes grew wide. His heart raced. He scrambled down the stairs still barefoot and flung open the front door just in time to see a fifteen-year-old Chinese Pistache topple out of his next door neighbor's front yard into the street.

"What the hell are you people doing!" he screamed over the loud grunts and whines of the saw. The crew was oblivious and rendered deaf with their sound-muffling ear protection. They didn't hear him approach.

The workers descended upon the tree collapsed on the pavement like a pack of jackals. They tore off its limbs and shoved them into the ravenous mouth of the hungry tree chipper parked in Alex's driveway.

Alex continued to yell and wave his arms wildly. The veins on the side of his neck contracted as his face grew a furious deep red.

"*Hey!* Turn that FRICKIN' thing off!" Alex caught the eye of the worker with the chain saw. The perplexed landscaper powered off the saw as the others stood in the street, momentarily ceasing their assault on the tree in the road.

"Who authorized this!" Alex demanded.

"Hey, man, we're just doing our jobs." The worker produced a an official looking piece of paper with a map of the neighborhood and a list of trees marked on it. "Just following orders, you know?"

At just this point, Raven pulled in and parked across the street. She sat in the car dumbfounded by the scene in front of her. The tree was sprawled out in the road with orange parking cones dotted around it. The roar of the huge red chipper was powering down as all the focus in the neighborhood was on Alex dressed in his sweats, standing barefoot in his neighbor's yard. He was waving and screaming at a guy holding a chain saw!

What happened next was the last thing she ever expected. Alex wrestled the chain saw out of the worker's hands and hurled it across the neighbor's yard!

Scene Twenty-Five: Just Following Orders

"Holy crap!" Raven gasped as she instinctively put her hands over her mouth. She could not believe this. In all the years she had known Alex, he had always been the most mild-mannered, easy-going, gentle, amiable, level-headed guy she had ever known. He had never shown any inclination towards violence. He was the type of guy who would always use his brains to negotiate a conflict. This was so profoundly out of character for him, Raven found herself checking for clues to be sure this really was the man she thought she knew. She recognized the glasses, the stocky build, the clothes looked familiar... it *sounded* like him...

Finally, she stepped out of the car to see if there was anything she could do to help. Alex was on his cell phone calling the homeowner's association as she walked up.

"Who authorized this?" he demanded. "Why weren't any of the homeowners notified? What is the reason for this?" A mumbled voice on the receiver gave some answers Alex did not find acceptable.

Apparently the tree had been targeted for destruction because its roots were causing a small lift of about three quarters of an inch in the neighbor's walkway. It was believed to be too great a risk. The tree was a legal "liability."

Raven found herself feeling everything from a very strange perspective of oneness. She felt Alex's anger, frustration, pain, and concern. She felt the worker's confusion and a hint of fear. Raven also felt a different sort of energy from the tree. After her experience in Yosemite, she felt even more deeply for the tree lying in the street. She knew it had its own unique kind of consciousness and life force. A living thing had been sacrificed for an errant piece of concrete that was going to get jack-hammered and re-poured in a few days anyway. This was senseless. Tragic.

Alex's neighbor, Jake, walked out completely stunned. Raven felt his reaction as well. Shock, anger, confusion. He was remaining calm but Raven could feel how much effort it was taking.

The association president, who lived in the neighborhood, walked up next with her dog on a leash. Both Alex and Jake set upon her with angry accusations.

"What the hell is going on here?!" they demanded in unison.

The association president explained what Alex had just heard over the phone. Her explanation was entirely fear-based, official-sounding bureaucratic compost.

There was nothing that could be done.

"What other trees are you taking out?!" Alex, still shaking with fury, wanted to know.

There was a cherry tree around the corner and another Chinese Pistache down the street. They had committed the same crime—dislodging cement. One was close to an electrical box, the other threatened a sewer pipe. It was hard to argue with either decision.

Raven found, to her surprise, she also empathized with the association president. She had been in a similar role years ago, and she knew exactly what this woman was dealing with. She was merely a puppet for a corporation that told her what needed to be done, and no one in the neighborhood even participated in association meetings.

In this moment, Raven experienced a strange epiphany. She could understand and have compassion for every single perspective involved in this situation. Every person, every position, every emotion was accessible and real to her. They were all equally real and valid. There was no "right and wrong" nor "good and evil." Everything just *was*, and she was able to be present to it.

The effect of this moment was startling. She suddenly grasped what it meant to be "in the world but not of it." She was fully present—feeling everything and holding a space of complete understanding for each person and even the fallen tree—yet not entangled in it.

Once again, she was reminded of what she learned in Yosemite. "No Greater. No Less. All One Love." Even in the midst of chaos and conflict, Raven was able to be a compassionate observer. She found this to be exactly what was needed in this situation.

Raven approached Alex and put her hand on his shoulder. He was still shaking with rage over this distressing event and she hoped she might be able to help calm him down.

"Well, this was quite a scene." she remarked.

"Did you see that? Did you see what they did?" Alex was waving his arms in the direction of the tree lying in the road. The

Scene Twenty-Five: Just Following Orders

chipper fired up again as the workers found another chain saw and got back to business.

"'*We were just following orders!*' the guy said. Do you know how many stupid, horrific events have gone down in human history on the basis of that one mindless irresponsible statement? The Holocaust? The Trail of Tears? Pol Pot? Somalia? Does anyone ever think for themselves? Will people do whatever they're told just to collect a paycheck? Doesn't anyone ever look at the big picture? Jake just lost a fifteen-year-old, beautiful tree that shaded his home and saves him money on air conditioning every summer and for what? His walkway had a little crack, a little lifted-up part? They're just trying to protect their asses from a lawsuit!" Alex was almost hyperventilating now.

"Easy there. Let's not add a heart attack to the excitement today, okay?" Raven just nestled in to Alex's arms and held him close. As his breathing slowed, she continued to silently pray and invite nurturing and protecting Mother energy into the situation.

"Not much more we can do here..." she finally said. "How about you get ready and we go get some food. We can talk about this over brunch."

Alex glared at the landscaping crew and walked stiffly back up his own walkway. Raven realized there was a lot more going on here than a neighborhood tree drama. She had a feeling whatever it was would be a clue to finding some resolution with Alex.

Scene Twenty-Six

Facing the Fear

"I just don't know what came over me. I've never lost it like that." Alex shook his head as he and Raven looked over the menus at their favorite café. "I thought they were coming for *my* tree. I remember when they showed up a couple of years ago and chopped down three redwoods right in my courtyard. Some idiot planted redwoods too close to the foundations, so they let them grow for thirteen years and then came out and hacked them all down. No one *thinks*, anymore. *Idiots!* It's like no one has any idea of the long term consequences of their actions."

Suddenly Raven saw how perfectly this event mirrored their relationship. They had been hasty in starting a business together before their relationship was really solid. They put a lot of financial stress on themselves. They had no idea what the long term consequences would be.

Today, they were at the same place the Chinese Pistache had been moments before the chain saw was revved up. Do we tear it down because it's tripping us up and a little inconvenient? How do we deal with the long term consequences—the wounds we've inflicted on each other's hearts? What are the long term consequences of ending this? What are the consequences of trying make it work?

Raven thought again of the tree lying in the street awaiting its fate in the jaws of the chipper. It felt like her heart was about to do the same. It made her sad. Now this was getting personal.

"So, what are you going to have?" Alex interrupted her reverie. Somehow a simple inquiry about her brunch selection seemed a whole lot weightier.

"Oh… um, I'm thinking maybe the fruit-stuffed French toast. That's pretty good stuff. Feeling like a little comfort food after all that, you know?"

"Tell me about it…" Alex continued to peruse the menu, obviously still distracted.

The waiter appeared to take their order. Alex made a quick decision to just "go with what she's having" and they were left with a clear table and looking at one another not knowing where to start.

"So, how did that Small Claims Court situation turn out? Did you win?" Alex inquired.

"Oh, yeah… It all worked out fine. The judge ruled in my favor and John owes me the rest of the money on the job." Raven offered.

It all seemed like a lifetime ago even though it had just happened last week. Raven realized how many conflicts she was having to navigate her way through lately. It was like there was some force in motion of almost hurricane proportions that was cleaning out the places in her life that needed it most. She wondered if the Master Key she had been working with had something to do with it. How could she possibly embody a symbol of healing and oneness and then live her life out of sync with that directive? It was impossible. She was having to change. She had to look fearlessly at every aspect that was out of alignment with Love and make the necessary corrections. It was all happening so fast… and she realized she was having to take responsibility for her part in each situation.

"You seem a bit distracted." Alex noticed. "What's on your mind?"

"Well… you know." Raven fidgeted with her coffee cup trying to find the words. "It's not so much what's on my mind… it's what's on my heart."

"Yeah, me too." Alex agreed. Neither of them wanted to say

Scene Twenty-Six: Facing the Fear

it. Neither wanted to go first. Raven did anyway.

"I've realized over the last few months a lot of what I really love and appreciate about you." Raven offered. Alex's mood brightened a bit. "I appreciate... the way we can talk about *anything*. You are curious and smart. You can see the big picture on the world. You have a really big heart..." Raven's throat tightened as she thought of Alex going ballistic over a fallen tree. She didn't know he had that kind of passion or concern in him. He had always been so reserved, so cool, so emotionally distant. She just recognized it was all a carefully crafted façade. He was tender under all of that. He could care. He might even fight for something that mattered. Raven hoped she still mattered.

"And I am also realizing that there are some things that *aren't* working between us. We keep beating each other up over the mistakes we've made in the past. Every time one of us screws up, the other one pulls out the rap sheet and rattles off all the prior offenses. We have got to find a way to forgive each other and move on... or we're just going to..."

"Move on." Alex completed her sentence.

"Yeah... exactly." Raven bit her lip. The waiter arrived with their food just entirely too cheerful for the conversation.

"And who ordered the fruit-stuffed French toast?" he joked lamely, knowing full well they had both ordered the same thing. "Here you go! Does anyone need more coffee?" Raven and Alex waived him off as he bounced off back to the kitchen.

"We have a lot of good stuff going on here." Alex continued. "It would be a shame to just chuck everything with all we've been through together. I really do care about you..." Alex poured syrup over his French toast. "It's just... I'm *afraid*. Honestly, that's it. I'm afraid of getting hurt. I've been through this kind of thing in the past... I put my heart on a platter for some woman and then she just..."

"Runs it through the wood chipper?" Raven completed his sentence.

Alex laughed uneasily. "Yeah. Actually... I can see the connection there."

"You know, I heard somewhere that anger is really just a

sign post for fear. When we're angry, we blame everyone else for their bad behavior, for their stupidity, for hurting us. It's easy to go to the 'victim' place and try to protect ourselves from more hurt."

"I think you're on to something. Go on." Alex was listening.

"Well, like the thing with the tree this morning. I've never seen you *that angry* before! Honestly, I didn't think you had that in you — who *was* that guy grabbing chain saws and hurling them across the yard?" Raven joked.

Alex blushed a little then mockingly beat his chest like a gorilla.

"Actually, it was kind of *hot* in a weird way." Raven winked.

"Now we're getting somewhere!" Alex smiled.

"Okay, but really. Back to the anger and fear thing."

"Darn" said Alex. "I was liking the hot thing."

Raven persisted. "So. You were really angry about the tree. It wasn't even *your* tree in *your* yard. You were taking the entire thing personally. Why do you think that was? I didn't have any idea until you just mentioned you thought they were coming for *your* trees. Why do you think that was so visceral for you? What does that tree outside your window represent to you?"

Alex thought for a moment. Then he thought for another moment. Finally, he seemed to actually connect to a very real feeling around all this.

"I look out that window every day when I'm working from my office at home. I've watched that tree grow from a little sapling with a pole tied to it to this big canopy that fills up my entire window. It's my 'tree house,' you know?" Alex's eyes were glistening as he really felt it. "That tree has been part of every year I've been building this business. When we broke up, I felt like you were taking an axe to what we built together, to the business we created. But I kept working. I kept building. I kept nurturing my business. And the tree was there the whole time—just growing right alongside me. It was *there*. Kind of my silent partner..."

Raven's heart was breaking as Alex continued.

"If they had cut that tree down this morning..."

Raven saw it now. The business was Alex's baby, his identity, his hope, his future. He put much more stock in it than she had. For

Scene Twenty-Six: Facing the Fear

her, it was just a means to an end—at best a form of self expression. For him, it was so much more. He was afraid of losing all he had worked so hard to create. He was afraid it was all just a big waste of time. He was afraid that on one careless morning, the business equivalent of a bunch of guys in hard hats would hack it all down and throw it in the wood chipper. He identified with the tree as a symbol for his business the way she just had for their relationship. She realized that to him, she was the one holding the chain saw. To her, he was the one throwing her heart in the chipper.

"I know…" Raven said quietly as she reached across the table and touched his hand. Somehow Alex knew that she did.

Scene Twenty-Seven

Into the Fire

"I've never asked you to change for me." Raven stated, defensively.

"And I've never asked you to *stop* changing." Alex was sincere.

They had been working intensively on their relationship for nearly a month now. Sometimes the conversations carried on face-to-face and heart-to-heart until late in the evening. Their discussion continued throughout the day with quick texts or e-mails blasting their spontaneous insights and relationship discoveries.

Today they were back at it.

"Are you saying that *I'm* the one who needed to do the most changing? Is that it? I'm a piece of work that really needed an overhaul?" Raven was getting agitated. This was a sore subject for her. She had invested enormous amounts of time, money, and energy on her own healing and personal development process. Alex had done very little, in her opinion, and it just seemed to make the chasm between them seem even greater.

"No. *No!* That's **not** what I meant. What I mean is that I accept you for who you are. You don't need to do anything to change or improve on who you are. You are this amazing, talented, brilliant, attractive, funny, loving, and always interesting woman. When are you going to just accept that? When are you just going to *be* and get off the hamster wheel of trying to better yourself? You're an artist—don't you always know when the art is 'done' and when it's time to just sit back and admire it?"

Raven could feel his love so intensely it almost burned. She realized that everything she put herself through was a journey into wholeness, into self-acceptance. If she really and truly believed the Divine completely and unconditionally loved her, and that her purpose was to embody love, then why was she holding out on acceptance for *herself*? Just as bad, why was she holding out on fully accepting Alex and his own process. It wasn't right to expect his journey to look exactly like hers. They each had their own ways of experiencing the world, their own lessons, their own issues to overcome.

Raven was silent as she allowed herself to really receive Alex's words. She let each word sink in, "amazing, talented, brilliant, attractive, funny, loving, and always interesting." Raven breathed them into her heart and made space for them. She allowed them in.

"How ironic." she thought, "Here I have exerted all this effort to try and love the whole world and I haven't gotten around to accepting this love for myself."

She looked into Alex's deep brown eyes. "And I haven't been giving it authentically to the one person who loves me most." Raven felt like a fraud. Ridiculous. All that work, all those years of healing, and here it was Alex who hadn't read a single book or attended a single workshop who was administrating her doctorate thesis in Love. This was all that mattered—*acceptance*.

"Thank you." Was all she could say. She really meant it. Raven excused herself to get some water.

Scene Twenty-Seven

When she returned, she brought back a stack of 3"x5" cards she pulled from her bag.

"You know, I've been thinking..." she started. "About that huge rap sheet of offenses we just keep pulling out and beating each other with..."

Alex looked intrigued. Raven continued,

"And I was thinking that I'm ready to let that stuff go..." her hands slid along the edges of the cards as she talked. "In fact, I'm ready to completely burn it up, make it disappear, never pull it out again... I'd like to wipe the slate clean and start over."

"I'd like that too." Alex agreed. "So, how do we do that?"

"Well, maybe you can indulge me in a little ceremony. I was thinking we could each write out everything we blame the other one for... everything we don't accept, every hurt we cling to... and put them on these cards."

Alex raised a single brow then smiled. Raven took that for a "yes."

Raven and Alex each retreated to a corner of the house with a stack of cards and a pen. They spent nearly thirty minutes writing out every grievance, every wound. By the time they were finished, they each held a stack nearly a quarter of an inch thick.

"I'll show you mine, if you show me yours." Alex teased.

"I think that will not be necessary." Raven asserted. "I don't want to re-hash or re-wound. We've spent a whole month chewing on this stuff. We know damn well what's on these cards."

"Agreed." said Alex.

"Okay, you go light the grill in the backyard. I'm going to pull a couple of things together for the ceremony." said Raven.

Alex rummaged through the garage for some briquettes and mesquite chips. While there, he discovered Raven's snow shoes.

"You want these at your place?" he shouted.

"Sure. Leave them out for me." Raven shouted back from the living room.

Alex stoked the grill in the backyard up to a respectable blaze. Raven collected three candles, one large white one and two smaller ones—one green, the other purple.

Raven placed the candles on the patio table and lit the two smaller ones, leaving the larger one for later.

"This represents you. This represents me." She pointed with the lighter to the candles.

They sat opposite one another with the blazing fire between them. The sparks and curling smoke rose into the pitch black night of the new moon.

"So. How about we do *this*..." Raven suggested. "We will each look at what we've written on the card, and without telling the other person what we wrote, take turns throwing our grievance into the fire. As I look at each card, I am acknowledging that I forgive you for this, and I also acknowledge that I forgive myself for the ways I have contributed to it or do the same thing myself. Basically, I cannot be bothered by something in you that does not already exist in myself. I am acknowledging that you are my perfect mirror. Sound good?"

"Sounds good." Alex agreed.

Raven looked at the first card in her stack. She allowed herself to feel it, to forgive it. She tossed it in the flame. The card caught fire, turned brown like a toasted marshmallow, then dissolved into grey and black flakes of ash. With each card that was to follow, a burst of flame surged skyward as she released its energy and its hold on the two of them.

Alex looked at his card and did the same. Back and forth they silently set aflame and released their hurts, their wounds, their anger, their resentments. They replaced each one with forgiveness of self and forgiveness of the other. It took nearly twenty minutes to get through both stacks.

When the last card went up in a glorious blaze and the ashes had begun to pile up, they decided to add something else to their ceremony.

"I think we should replace all that crap with what we would *rather* create." Alex suggested.

"Excellent." Raven agreed. "Would you like to go first?"

Alex was speaking directly from his heart.

"I want to replace competition with cooperation."

Scene Twenty-Seven

"And I want to replace judgment with acceptance." said Raven.
"Let's replace blame with responsibility." added Alex.
"And selfishness with support." Raven offered.
"Speaking of that… there's something I wanted to share with you…" Alex reached into his pocket and pulled out a folded piece of paper. "You know how you tell me you wish you saw more of my tender side? Well, I wrote this for you…" Raven sat quietly and let his poem embrace her.

Between Two Worlds

Afraid to fly too high
The sun might melt the wings
That keep me in the sky

Afraid to go too low
I might never fly again
Trapped on the earth below

Stuck in a place between the light
between heaven and Earth
between past and future
between black and white

Angelic messenger in both worlds
Yet belonging in neither
Can I enjoy this present moment
A "fleeting" now that may last forever

Can I learn the lessons this time
Know that I am more than enough
Believe that I am whole
Even when life is rough

Can I see the talents within others
Appreciate them well
Accept their gifts
As I would a bouquet of flowers

Can I be a good leader
Benevolent in my intention
and a faithful servant
Kind and humble in my ascension

Can I learn to play with others
Let go of my tears... and fears
Learn to love my sisters and brothers

Here I stand on the shore
Looking at the sea
Destined to be ...
the best I can be

Alex slowly folded the paper back up as Raven wiped runny tears from her cheeks and sniffed.

"Don't you dare throw *that* in the fire!" Raven exclaimed between sobs. "That was beautiful..." For the first time in their relationship, she felt seen. She felt heard.

They stood from their seats facing one another. Raven and Alex embraced as the flames died down and the ashes scattered on the evening breeze. In between gentle kisses the banter continued.

"I love you." admitted Alex.

"I love you, too." admitted Raven.

"So, was that hot?" asked Alex.

"Very hot. Set-the-world-on-fire hot, in fact." laughed Raven.

They turned around and each of them picked up a smaller candle sitting on the patio table.

"Here's to no more separation." said Raven as they each touched their flames to the large white candle.

"So, you really thought that was hot?" asked Alex.

Raven just laughed. "You really are such a simple creature, aren't you? Yes. I loved it. Let's go inside."

Section Four

Onward and Outward

Scene Twenty-Eight

Sanctuary of Grandmothers

Emotionally exhausted from her marathon reconciliation with Alex, Raven looked forward to her monthly meeting of the Grandmothers and the nurturing safety of mostly female company.

Raven was an unlikely "Grandmother." Many of the women in the Grandmothers group were not even mothers, much less old enough to have grandchildren. The name of the group was not derived from their familial status as actual grandmothers, but rather inspired by the books and message of Sharon McErlane, author of *A Call to Power: The Grandmothers Speak*. Their focus each month was bringing harmony to the world by balancing yin (feminine) and yang (masculine) energies. The group worked with a concept they called The Net of Light to infuse loving intention into the world and ease the transformation process for humanity and the Earth.

Those who attended the monthly gathering sought to be a positive force for change in the world by embodying love, compassion, gratitude, and true feminine power. Raven found The Grandmothers a haven of strength and light in a world often frantic with fear and chaos. She enjoyed the diversity of the group's members—women and men, all ages, all ethnicities, all traditions of spiritual practice. The common bond was simple—love.

Raven noticed the predominant energy she experienced in the group was the nurturing and supportive Mother energy she invited in her meditations. The energy was as vast, strong, and nurturing as her experience of the Yosemite Valley.

At today's meeting, Raven arrived early and for the first time since she had begun attending had some time to chat with Eve.

Eve hosted the monthly Sacramento Grandmothers meeting. Her cozy suburban home featured a large meandering backyard where fountains, walkways, assorted crystals, wind chimes, fruit trees, and a vegetable garden beckoned visitors to be still and enjoy the sacred space. It was no wonder Eve called the space "The Sanctuary."

Eve herself was light-hearted and quick to find amusement in even the deepest topics. Raven imagined that a woman much like her could have been her mother's roommate in college. Her long flowing dark hair, knowledge of animal totems, beaded medicine pouch around her neck, and familiarity with Native American prophecies led Raven to believe she may have some indigenous ancestry. She was as difficult to pin down on her heritage as Raven had been for Karly. It turned out Eve knew many *other* things as well.

"So I hear you are working with some sort of symbol, and that you might need to go to Maui with it."

Eve startled Raven with both her knowing and directness. She also reminded Raven that she hadn't thought much about the Master Key or her task in several months with all the drama going on with a court case and a relationship rescue. The Master Key appeared to be clearing out and healing its own "backyard" (Raven) before tending to the rest of the world.

Raven realized that her friend Pat, who first invited her to the group, must have told Eve about the Master Key. Pat had a reputation among them as "the connector" and here was further proof of her gift in action.

At one time, Raven thought she might need to travel to Hawaii to do similar work to what she did in Yosemite. Lately, however, she wasn't so sure. Maybe it was just a longing for her birth home. Raven's memories of the islands were as faded as the Polaroids taken there when she was two.

Scene Twenty-Eight: Sanctuary of Grandmothers

"Um, yes. Apparently, I have encoded within my energetic field a symbol that I need to get out to the world. I've been told it will help in raising human consciousness." Raven surprised herself with her own audacious transparency. The words escaped from her mouth like a beach ball that could no longer be held underwater. Raven was actually a bit relieved to say the words out loud and not be ridiculed. Part of her still half-expected to be chased by an angry mob with torches and pitch forks and boiled in oil. For some reason, she felt safe with Eve.

"Oh, yes. There it is!" Eve observed Raven clairvoyantly and could actually see the symbol emerging from her heart chakra. "It's a playful little thing, isn't it? Hello there!" Eve waved playfully at something several inches from Ravens chest. " So, what do you call this symbol of yours?"

"We've been calling it the Master Key. It's based on sacred geometry and contains 144 nodes on 12 rays wrapped around a sphere. Each node corresponds to a color of the light spectrum and follows the Fibonacci sequence or Divine proportion." Again, Raven was amazed at how much she felt comfortable sharing with Eve.

"Yes. I see that. So... how are you working with it? What does it *do*?" Eve inquired.

"That is a *very* good question..." Raven admitted. "I have been getting some very strong Guidance lately that rather than taking it to Maui, I actually need to make a trip to Mount Shasta. My birthday happens to correspond with the shift on the Mayan calendar from Galactic to Universal Consciousness on 2-11-11. I'm getting a very strong impression I need to be somewhere powerful to 'upload' this symbol... someplace with a strong energy... a 'portal' if you will."

Eve had the same introspective look on her face Raven recognized from observing Susan Rueppel. She paused, listening to a quiet voice from deep within.

"Yes. You *do*. And Shasta is an excellent place for you to go! I'm seeing *waterfalls*... Something you need to do up there has to do with blessing and healing the water. The water will flow out in every direction charged with this healing energy of the Master Key through the rivers, the streams, the creeks, even the evaporation and rainfall. Did you know the headwaters of the Sacramento River are at the base of Mount Shasta?"

"No. I'm not really up on those kinds of things." Raven admitted. "But this gives me something interesting to check with Guidance."

"This time of year will be tricky getting to the falls. Most of them are only accessible by *snow shoes!*" Eve laughed as she said this, thinking it unlikely Raven would be equipped for such a spontaneous adventure.

"Actually… you are not going to believe this… I *have* a pair of snow shoes in the trunk of my car!" Raven laughed.

"What are the odds of that?!" Eve laughed harder. "Well, that settles it. Just ask which falls you're supposed to visit and you're set."

As they talked, Raven realized that Eve was giving her some of the clues she had been seeking. Just as The General had told her in Mariposa Grove, she was getting exactly the information she needed and not a moment before she needed it. Raven realized there was one more component to all of this and Eve might have some information for her.

"OK, so here's something…" Raven continued, "The Monday right after my birthday I'm going with my friend Susan to San Francisco for a business meeting. Anything hit you about that?"

Eve's eyes brightened, then she looked a bit confused. "OK… I'm seeing one of those… what do you call them?… like that big tall monument in DC…"

"Like the Washington Monument?" Raven interjected.

"Yes! Like that!"

"Well, San Francisco has a building that looks a lot like that—The Transamerica Building."

"Yep. That's it! I see you doing something with the Master Key and the Transamerica Building."

Raven had no idea what to say. This was so random Eve might as well have told her to go bless all the money in the Federal Reserve Building while she was in town. It was so random, in fact, there might actually be something to it.

Scene Twenty-Eight: Sanctuary of Grandmothers

Raven had been so immersed in her conversation with Eve, she hadn't noticed the rest of the group had settled in to the living room and were ready to begin the meeting.

"Thanks, Eve. I'll see what I can find out about the water falls and the Transamerica Building before I go to Shasta."

"Have fun!" Eve smiled. "Let me know how it goes."

Raven was grateful for Eve's timely information, and once again reminded that feminine energy, the Divine Feminine, was all about ease and grace. Nothing about her task needed to be difficult or complicated. It did not even need to be fully understood to be powerful and effective. All she needed was the willingness to do her part. Something Susan had said in one of her consultations suddenly had much greater meaning, "You have all the help you will ever need."

Scene Twenty-Nine

GPS:
Guidance, Pre-Shasta

"Obelisks and waterfalls..." Raven pondered aloud from her leather recliner, her feet stretched out on the ottoman in her living room. Looking across the room to the bookcase, her eyes stumbled across the citrine obelisk placed among the Platonic solids.

"I wonder..." she said to Isis.

The cat looked up from nibbling its paws. Her toes were splayed out from her hind leg in another bizarre kitty yoga position Raven had dubbed "Leopard Plays the Banjo." The feline paused and stared with wide eyes, as if anticipating Raven's next comment.

Raven pulled out her laptop and queried the search engine for information about the Transamerica building in San Francisco. Her eyes skimmed across the text on her screen until two construction facts caught her attention.

"The building's façade is covered in crushed quartz, giving the building its pure white color." And "The aluminum cap is indirectly illuminated from within to balance the appearance at night."

Raven looked at the crystal obelisk sitting on the bookcase, then back at the words on her screen. She startled Isis out of her Banjo pose.

"*The whole building is a giant hard drive!* They covered it in crushed quartz!"

As Raven said these words out loud, she immediately perceived that the building could be "charged" just like any other crystal. An image, a precognition perhaps, flashed in her mind of her walking up to the building and placing her hand on its crystal covered base.

"If the vibration was powerful enough, the quartz on the building would store that information within its crystalline structure, just like a massive hard drive would store a software program." she thought.

"So, I wonder what the deal is with the aluminum cap pyramid at the top?"

Raven ran another search engine query. "Aluminum" produced an abundance of information. Most of what turned up would be helpful for a chemistry class report. Nothing caught her attention until…

"Aluminium is capable of being a superconductor…"

Raven clicked the link on "superconductor."

"…superconductivity is a quantum mechanical phenomenon…"

Two more clicks led her to a term she had heard once while watching The Science Channel at Alex's place —"Quantum Entanglement."

"Entanglement is that strange quantum phenomenon that links two particles across distances such that any measurements carried out on one particle immediately changes the properties of the other—even if they are separated by the entire universe. Einstein called it 'spooky action at a distance."

Raven bookmarked the quantum entanglement link; for some reason it seemed important.

Letting these seemingly random facts perform their alchemical dance in her mind, Raven felt another idea surface. She stared at the screen in disbelief.

"If the building is covered in quartz crystal and has an aluminum cap, then the Transamerica Building is a perfectly engineered *broadcast station* for the energy of the Master Key! It would not only store the energy within its natural crystalline façade, but it could *transmit* the signal on a quantum mechanical level to millions

Scene Twenty-Nine: GPS—Guidance, Pre-Shasta

of people.

"Okay, now I'm *really* curious…" she thought.

Raven searched again. This time the query was for "Washington Monument."

"**Constructed of marble, granite, and blue gneiss…**"

Raven pulled out her *Definitive Guide to Crystals* to discover that marble was a combination of calcite and dolomite. Calcite was listed as being a "powerful amplifier and cleanser of energy."

Raven read further.

"**Pyramidal point was cast by William Frishmuth from aluminum…**"

"They are both made from materials that store and amplify energy, and they both have these superconductor aluminum caps…"

"They are *all connected*." Raven revisited the definition of quantum entanglement.

…any measurements carried out on one particle immediately changes the properties of the other—even if they are separated by the entire universe…

"There is a reason both the ancient and modern structures are constructed from similar materials. It's like they were *designed* to be compatible! They function as a network just like our modern cellular towers. Only these obelisks are connected *energetically*. The superconductor caps link them in a quantum way by means of entanglement. It's the ultimate wi-fi network!"

Raven was still processing her discovery about the obelisks, when she remembered that she was going to Mount Shasta the day before her trip to San Francisco with Susan. Now that she understood the clue about "obelisk" she needed to understand what "waterfall" was all about.

Time to ask for guidance about her visit to Shasta. She set her computer on the floor then settled back into her recliner. Raven took a deep breath, invited the Light into her crown chakra and prayed, "Please guide me."

She waited within the silence until her body and thoughts were at rest. Soon, an image appeared in her mind.

She saw herself hiking along a path near a river. In several places, she stopped to meditate. Before each meditation, she watched herself perform a brief shamanic ceremony. There were candles of very specific colors facing specific directions, she was shaking a rattle made from the shell of a turtle, with a small bowl of sage burning to cleanse the area around her.

"When did I get a shaman's license?" Raven wondered. She had learned by now that nothing this specific was given to her by chance. Raven wrote what she saw down in her green leather journal.

Returning to her meditation, Raven noted that she was chanting specific phrases from the Aramaic prayer and gifting the Master Key at each location, much as she had done in Yosemite.

"Well, this is quite the universal ceremony!" she thought. "By the time I'm done, I will have included several of the Kabbalist 72 Names of God, the Aramaic Lord's Prayer, and an entire native American offering to every direction and dimension. I guess it makes sense—the Master Key is *Universal*—all beings in all times and all dimensions."

Raven reached again for her laptop and found a trail guide for the Mount Shasta region. She asked for guidance as to which waterfalls she was supposed to visit. One in particular stood out.

"**McCloud Falls... three waterfalls a short distance apart. This time of year, they can only be reached with snow shoes. Visitors need to register by permit with the Ranger's station.**"

The description fit everything she had either heard or intuited.

"McCloud Falls it is." Raven thought as she checked online to get driving directions. She marveled at the strange intersection in which she had just found herself—experiencing intuitive guidance working seamlessly with modern technology. Everything was unfolding in present time—moment by moment. Every answer available exactly when she needed it.

"GPS." Raven giggled to herself. "Guidance—Pre-Shasta."

Scene Thirty

The Road to Shasta

Raven astonished her friends with an unusual request for her birthday. "Let's get together the *following* week. I'm spending the day snow-shoeing in Shasta."

In spite of their concerns about a solitary woman taking off to meander the wilderness alone, no one seemed to mind. She was, after all, the one known to take off to Yosemite alone for three days. To them, it was all just part of her "nature girl" persona. Raven didn't tell anyone the real purpose of her visit. Her "secret mission" was just too weird to explain to most people.

For Raven, this birthday was unique. She wasn't hitting a decade marker or any of the usual qualifiers for a watershed year. This birthday was February 11, 2011. This one fell on the precise date Calleman extrapolated to be the beginning of the Universal Underworld on the Mayan calendar. Her birthday aligned with what many believed would be the tipping point in shifting human consciousness[1].

1: This date was cited in Calleman's book *The Mayan Calendar and the Transformation of Consciousness*. At the time many people, including Calleman, had changed the date to March 9, 2011 as the official beginning of the Universal Underworld. The Divine timing was still perfect, however.

Raven reflected on all of this as she set out early this Friday morning and drove north up Interstate 5. In the trunk of her car was a pair of snowshoes, her hiking boots, a day pack and her favorite walking stick.

The backpack contained a cloth drawstring bag which served as a medicine bag for the beautiful turtle rattle she had found at an authentic Native American Trading Post. This sacred object had a handle crafted from the hoof of a deer, a turtle's shell for the rattle chamber, and was accentuated with a ruff of fox fur and the feathers of hawk, raven, and a few coarse strands from a horse's mane.

Raven spent the afternoon prior to her departure preparing the various sacred objects she had been guided to bring on her journey. Guidance had sent her to the banks of the American River, where she selected four smooth river rocks about the size of her palm. On each stone she inscribed two of the ancient Kabbalah 72 Names of God. One of the Hebrew letter combinations was for "Water." Invoking this Name acknowledged the Light of God made manifest in the physical world. It promoted healing from within through one of the most vital and pervasive elements unique to planet Earth—water. The other Hebrew letter combination she inscribed on the stones was "Global Transformation." Invoking this Name acknowledged that change in the external world begins with personal transformation.

Raven's intention for this series of ceremonies was to heal and purify both the internal and external aspects of her world. She had been operating for some time now with the belief that she was a microcosm of the macrocosm. That is, she believed that transforming herself was her way of helping to transform the world.

While at the river, she performed a blessing ceremony with the turtle rattle to thank the animals that had given themselves or parts of themselves to create this sacred object. She thanked the ancestors and Mother Earth for their roles in tomorrow's ceremony and their guidance and presence in preparing for it. Raven burned a small cluster of the white sage and cleansed the energies of all the objects she would take to Shasta. She invited the presence of the Grandmothers to assist her with this ritual and keep her in accordance with the traditional and sacred rites. In spite of the fact she had no background or experience in any indigenous tradition, she somehow just seemed to know what to do. Something about the nature of this journey was different from her other experiences. Raven understood that she would need to adapt and respect what was needed. She reminded herself it was more important to do an imperfect ritual with a great heart than a perfect ritual with no heart.

As Raven thought about the ceremonies planned for her day in Shasta, she remembered how many of her regression sessions had been to roles as priests, shamans, medicine men or women, rabbis, or clerics. She felt as if all the knowledge and experience of so many diverse expressions of connecting with the Divine were still active within her cellular memory banks. Whenever the information was needed, the dormant cellular memory activated and unlocked precisely whatever she needed to know. More and more, Raven found she "knew" without "knowing." She was learning to trust it.

After nearly four hours of driving past farmland, orchards, rest stops and truck stops, Raven finally glimpsed the snow-covered peak of Mount Shasta on the horizon. She had never visited Shasta before and was making an effort to just experience it for herself. Over the years, Raven had heard more New Age folk tales about Shasta than the Brothers Grimm could hope to create under the influence of psychotropics.

Depending on whom you talked to, there were aliens cloaked (or abducting people) in the lenticular clouds that routinely formed around its peak. Others believed an ancient race of technologically advanced beings lived deep inside the mountain, waiting for their cue to reveal themselves to humanity at the appropriate moment. They were holding out until humans evolved enough to not fear them; or worse, cast them in a reality TV show.

What Raven heard that resonated most was the nature of the *energy* at Shasta. With each mile she traveled closer to the mountain, Raven noticed a certain feeling flow through her. The energy, as she experienced it, was… *accelerating*. An image of the spazzy, whirling Tasmanian Devil cartoon character came immediately to mind. The energy of Shasta felt like she had been thrown into a centrifuge in a biology laboratory. Raven suspected that if she stayed here long enough, all the density would soon spin right out of her.

The other quality she quickly discerned was Shasta's energy of *amplification*. Raven noticed a feeling of expansion and rapid growth. It felt like being a balloon stretched in every direction all at once.

Raven imagined herself leaving this place like an over-inflated balloon with the end left open—accelerating around in dizzying circles only to collapse with a "plop" on the ground. She wondered how people could live here, blasting themselves in this hurricane of energy day after day. Raven recognized that the energy felt entirely different in Shasta than Yosemite. Where the Yosemite valley was powerfully feminine and nurturing, Shasta was masculine and energizing.

"Why would I need to come here? And why would I need to come here *now*, right before my trip to San Francisco?" Raven wondered. It was certainly not the flavor of energy she most preferred, but Guidance was Guidance. Right now she wished Guidance had picked Maui.

Turning off the interstate, Raven pulled into the small town of Shasta City. A strange mix of New Age rock shops, yoga centers, and body workers resided side by side with pizza parlors, gun shops, and mechanics. After a quick bite at a roadside café, Raven drove to the headwaters of the Sacramento River. This would be her first ceremonial stop.

Scene Thirty-One

Chasing Waterfalls

The headwaters were not at all what Raven expected. Tucked away in a nondescript park near the edge of town, a steady stream of ice-cold water no more than eight feet wide poured out from an underground cavern at the base of the mountain.

Glistening across bright green moss, the water was shallow enough she could have waded across and not even immersed her hips. It was cold enough that she wouldn't think of it.

Raven sat down on a grassy spot near the water's edge and pulled the medicine bag from her pack. This would be the simplest and shortest ceremony of the day, but it needed to be given the right intention and respect. Reaching down into the bag, she pulled out one of the smooth stones she had inscribed with the Hebrew 72 Names of God for "Water" and "Global Transformation." Closing her eyes, she meditated and brought forth the energy of the Master Key out from her heart chakra, through her arms, and into her hands. As her hands blazed with intense heat, the stone began to grow warm within her palm. She visualized the energy of the Master Key charging the stone and amplifying the energy of the Names inscribed upon it.

Raven voiced her intentions, that the stone and its energies be gifted to Mother Earth and to this water—her vital bloodstream.

She also asked that her gift bless everything and everyone the water touched in all its many forms—water, vapor, and rain. When she had finished charging the stone with its blessing, Raven stood and tossed the stone into the icy stream.

"One down, three to go…"

Within twenty minutes Raven reached the trail head for McCloud Falls. Raven parked a half mile from the Lower Falls campground and prepared for her first hike. As expected, the ground was over a foot deep in Spring snow and her snow-shoes were exactly what the Universe had ordered.

Donning water-resistant hiking pants, a fleece jacket, and her hiking boots, Raven fastened on her snow-shoes. The day pack swung light and easy out of the trunk and onto her back. All it contained were items for the ceremony, a few snacks for the trail and her water system.

She pulled the walking stick out and clomped down the trail to see a wooden park sign directing her to Lower Falls. Following the river, she *heard* Lower Falls well before seeing it.

Raven hiked until she found a place where she could remove her snow-shoes and set up her space for the ceremony. Upstream a couple took pictures of the falls and downstream two men set up a tripod to do likewise.

While Raven was a little relieved to see other people out by the river, she was also not inclined to make a scene. She suspected a woman shaking a turtle rattle, chanting and burning sage and candles in a state park might invite the wrong kind of attention. Raven waited. She pulled out her blanket and just spent some time at the river's edge grounding and meditating until the photographers decided to move on.

When she saw the last person hike back up the trail, Raven pulled out the contents of her medicine bag. She lit the sage and cleansed the energy of the space. She chanted the prayers she had been given by Guidance accompanied by the turtle rattle. Finally, she lit the appropriate colored candle for each direction.

Raven spent some time charging the smooth stone with the Hebrew

Scene Thirty-One: Chasing Waterfalls

letters inscribed on it. Once again, she brought forth the energy of the Master Key from her heart chakra and infused it into the stone. When the stone grew warm from the heat of her hands, she spent some time visualizing the vibrations of healing and wholeness expanding from the stone into the water that would soon flow over it. Raven stood and tossed the charged stone into the surging waters.

"Two down. Two to go...", she thought. "But first, I'd like to really enjoy this place and get a few pictures." Raven hiked to the observation platform above Lower Falls. She stood for some time to feel the misty spray of the water against her face and the sunlight warming her skin. She enjoyed the musical rush and roar of the waterfall as it echoed off the boulders and flirted with the branches of overhanging pines.

What surprised Raven most about every step of this journey was its pristine simplicity. She wondered if she was leaving out something important or if she was "doing it right." At this moment the voice of Guidance was clear,

"*Every good thing is simple. Enjoy it. Keep it that way.*"

"Good enough." thought Raven. She set out for her next location —Middle Falls.

The hike to Middle Falls was at least double the distance Raven had covered to get to Lower Falls. The view was worth it. The trail threaded in and out between pine trees and boulders like a stitched seam along the river's bank. Except for two other hikers who passed her going the opposite direction, Raven had all of this beauty completely to herself.

As she drew closer to Middle Falls, the sound of rushing water became deeper and louder. This waterfall was clearly much bigger than the one she had just left. Raven knew this long before it ever came into view.

Middle Falls presented an interesting challenge for a person here on a ceremonial mission. There was no place near the bottom of the falls to sit and meditate without blocking the trail or taking a very cold swim. Raven noticed the trail continuing up a narrow switchback series of steps.

"Nowhere to go but *up* from here." She thought to herself and smiled. Grateful for her walking stick, Raven ascended the extra quarter mile that zigzagged up the steep mountainside. When she reached the top, she gasped.

"Unbelievable." she said aloud.

There below her, she could see not only the falls, but the expanse of river that fed it. She found herself feeling suspended in air as if she were flying. The only thing above her from this lofty perch was the sky itself. She looked around and noticed a sandy clearing behind an outcropping of gnarled and twisted Manzanita bushes.

Raven set down her pack, set up her blanket, and prepared the ceremonial objects as before. She performed the same rites with the sage, the turtle rattle, and the candles. This time she gifted the Master Key not only to the stone she had brought along but to the whole of Mount Shasta. The mountain from this vantage point was directly behind her to the northeast and framed her like an ancient Egyptian priest performing ceremony beneath a pyramid.

As Raven completed her meditation, she opened her eyes to see a solitary butterfly waft past and land on the Manzanita bush directly in front of her.

"Transformation." Raven acknowledged. "Thank you…" she said to the butterfly. The butterfly lingered, winking with its fragile blue wings a subtle "thumbs up" from Mother Nature.

Raven gathered her things and hiked back to the bottom of the steep trail. The trail to Upper Falls was so buried in snow it could not even be detected, so she decided she must have gone as far as she was meant to go for the day. When she reached the trail adjacent to Middle Falls, Raven tossed the round stone she had charged with the Master Key into the rushing water.

"Mission accomplished." She smiled and took a deep breath. Walking back up the trail to her car, she noted the smell of pine needles and of moist earth saturated from snow. She delighted in the sounds of water racing past her and smashing into nearby boulders before careening through unchallenged stretches of icy rapids.

As she hiked along, she hummed a happy tune. It sounded a lot like *"Happy Birthday to You."*

Scene Thirty-Two

Return of the Phoenix

"Rain. Rain. And more rain." Raven commented to Susan as they sped down I-80 towards San Francisco. "I can't believe that in Shasta just a few days ago it was all clear blue and sunny skies... and now look at it!"

"I'm just glad we left as early as we did..." Susan noted. "So, how was your snow-shoe trip? Tell me all about it."

Raven filled Susan in on the ceremonies at the falls and how she had been tipped off by Eve about not only the waterfalls but the obelisks as well. She recounted what she discovered in her online research about the obelisk construction of quartz and granite... and the aluminum pyramid caps.

"Interesting..." Susan seemed to be taking it all in, seeing if there was any other insight she may need to add to the mix. She was, after all, the one who first informed Raven of her role with the Master Key.

"So, it looks like after we finish our meetings today, we need to pay a little visit to our favorite Northern California obelisk. It's only four blocks from the office where we'll be." Raven suggested.

"Sure. We can do that." Susan agreed.

"Isn't it interesting that of all the days we could be headed to San Francisco for a meeting, the only day that worked in everyone's schedule was February 14th?" Raven reflected. "Here we're going to upload the Transamerica Building with the energy of the Master Key, and quite possibly broadcast Love to every direction and dimension, and it's on *Valentine's Day*."

"You've always noticed the Master Key has both impeccable timing and a sense of humor." Susan noted with a smile.

"Yes. Yes it does." Raven agreed.

The rain pummeled down in relentless sheets and saturated Raven and Susan as they emerged at 2:30 PM from their two appointments. They had spent the last four hours working their magic, doing their combination Business Intuition and Soul Print sessions for several of Raven's colleagues. Their plan was to get feedback for their new service and test its viability for the corporate market. With their official business now behind them, they were free to run this strangely divine errand.

With just one small umbrella between them, they decided to take a cab. In moments, they splashed through the flooded gutter to the curb outside the iconic structure that defined the San Francisco skyline.

"I wonder if we can go up inside." Susan said.

"I don't think so. It's been off limits to everyone but tenants and their guests since 9/11." Raven offered. Sure enough, the security officer disguised as the lobby's front desk attendant was quick to suggest other destinations for tourists looking for a view.

"OK. Thanks!" Raven waved off the attendant as they went back outside to the sidewalk.

"We didn't need to go inside for what I need to do anyway." Raven reassured Susan. "The quartz is all on the *outside*."

Raven and Susan walked around to the side of the building and noticed a park full of redwood trees nestled between the Transamerica Building and the nearest lot. They noticed a wrought iron gate left slightly open. Fountains sprayed playful streams of water around whimsical metal frog sculptures in the park. It was

Scene Thirty-Two: Return of the Phoenix

probably a very refreshing and delightful effect when you were not already standing in a rainstorm. The massive redwoods shielded the worst of the rainfall, however.

At this moment, Raven's Guidance showed her an image of her walking over to one of the redwood trees and placing her hand on the tree. She knew that she needed to first gift the Master Key through the trees and seek their assistance to ground the energy deep into the earth through their root system.

Raven stepped up to the redwood and placed her right hand on its rough red bark. It reminded her immediately of its cousins at Mariposa Grove in Yosemite. She knew that if she could speak telepathically to the trees in Yosemite, she could do it again here.

"I have a gift I would like to give you. If you will accept my gift, I need for you to send it down into the earth through your roots. Will you accept my gift?"

"*Yes. I will do as you ask.*" The tree seemed to say from within Raven's mind.

Raven summoned the Master Key from her heart chakra and felt it surge through her arm into her hand. In her mind's eye she saw it travel down through the redwood's trunk and root system and into the earth all around the building.

"You must have strong roots before you can touch the sky!" Raven could almost hear the General all the way from Yosemite.

"OK." Raven turned to Susan trying to look casual while she was conversing with trees in the middle of a downpour. "Now the building and we're done."

The two of them stepped back out through the wrought iron gate away from the courtyard with the froggy fountains.

Raven stepped up to the quartz crystal encrusted pillar, look a deep breath, and closed her eyes. She prayed silently her ancient Aramaic prayer. Translated, it meant, "To You belongs the visioning power to guide the cosmos, the life energy to accomplish your plan, and the harmonious song — from gathering to gathering."

Raven once again brought forth the energy of the Master Key from her heart chakra, felt it surge through her right arm into her hand...

What happened next astonished Raven more than any of the amazing things she had yet experienced.

A part of her consciousness, perhaps her soul or etheric body seemed to detach itself from her physical body for a few moments. Raven experienced herself as pure energy flying up the crystal coated structure of the Transamerica Building. She was aware of her energy surging powerfully into every inch of the building's surface, and rocketing straight to the top where the aluminum pyramid cap awaited.

She felt herself come to a momentary halt, like a dragonfly hovering over a reed in a pond. She saw herself sitting at the top of the building, holding the massive Master Key sphere of energy in her hands like an oversized holographic beach ball.

No sooner had she taken notice of her perch than she felt herself speeding behind the giant Master Key through the air—the heading was due East. Raven sensed an almost magnetic pull guiding the Master Key from under the ground below. Intuitively she recognized it as a ley line, part of the energy grid that flows between sacred spaces and places of energetic power. They came to a sudden stop just above the Washington Monument!

Raven watched as the Master Key hovered above it and then dropped down from the top all the way to the bottom like the Times Square ball every New Year's Eve. The energy descended into the ground and dissipated.

Not yet completely back in her body, Raven marveled at the images she observed next.

Remembering what she had read about quantum entanglement, Einstein's "spooky action at a distance", she saw herself standing next to an ancient obelisk in the middle of a desert. In the same moment her hand had touched the Transamerica Building, she saw herself touching not only this obelisk, but every other obelisk of similar construction throughout the world. She sensed herself as being truly quantum in nature — simultaneously present in every time and dimension. The Universal energy of the Master Key, amplified and accelerated by her visit to Shasta, had connected the entire network.

Scene Thirty-Two: Return of the Phoenix

The feeling emitting from the obelisks was pure Love, and it washed over her in waves of joy.

She might have stayed to enjoy this celestial celebration all afternoon, had it not been for the fact her earthly body was getting drenched on the sidewalk and about to capture the attention of a security camera.

Raven fully returned to her physical body and opened her eyes to see Susan smiling on the other side of the pillar.

"You really shot up there, didn'tcha?" she said.

"You *saw* that?" Raven wondered.

"Uh huh."

"Do you think it *took?*" Raven asked.

"Oh yeeeeeaaaah." Susan confirmed.

"I'm soaked! Let's get a cab!" Raven suggested.

Just like that, in under ten minutes on a soggy sidewalk in San Francisco, the Phoenix had returned. At this point, no one knew the cosmic significance of what had just occurred, including the Phoenix herself.

Scene Thirty-Three

Connections

"Happy Birthday, Raven!"

One by one, Karly, Bennu, Susan, and Alex greeted Raven as they entered Old Soul with cards, hugs, and small gifts to celebrate.

Raven got an extra long hug from Alex, and a kiss.

"Well, I got something *extra special* for you this year. I hope it makes up for being clueless the last few birthdays. By the way, I got one for myself, too…

Alex handed Raven a slim, beautifully wrapped box about the size of thick notebook.

"An iPad2®! Well, you certainly know the way to this woman's heart!" Raven exclaimed.

"Gee, and I just brought chocolate." Karly joked.

"And I brought jewelry." Bennu added.

"You've both covered the only other real needs in my life." Raven jested back. "Don't sell yourself short. You both got out a lot cheaper, and it's every bit as much appreciated."

"You mean I could have just got you chocolate or jewelry? That would have saved me a whole lot of money." said Alex.

"No, you couldn't have. But they can." Raven put her arm around Alex's waist and snuggled in to his chest.

"Right." Alex sighed. "I guess I had a few back payments in there."

Raven started unpacking the iPad2® to test the wi-fi.

"I pre-charged it for you…" Alex noted.

"What a guy. Thinks of everything." Raven smiled up through her bangs as she crumpled up the wrapping paper. Alex meandered over to introduce himself to Susan and left Raven with Bennu and Karly. Bennu had been dying to ask,

"So, Raven, tell us about your birthday Shasta trip. How was the snow-shoeing?"

"Well, it was amazing… and very relaxing…" Raven was quickly trying to decide what she wanted to share. Bennu was current with everything—The Master Key, what she had learned from Susan, Yosemite, the whole crazy story. It was always Bennu that seemed to spur her on and really understand what went on in Raven's vast inner world. Karly, however, could end up going a lot of directions with this. Raven decided to risk it and divulge the whole thing. It was just too amazing to keep it to herself any longer. Raven looked primarily at Bennu and figured she'd let Karly come along for the ride.

"Well, turns out the whole purpose of the Shasta trip was to prepare me for going to San Francisco with Susan a couple of days ago." Raven began.

"I went first to the headwaters and did a ceremony with the water there, and then went to the falls at McCloud and did another ceremony there. I made it on my snow-shoes to the Lower Falls and the Middle Falls. I couldn't get anywhere near the Upper Falls, the trail was completely snowed over."

Bennu completely understood what all that meant and Karly would never admit she didn't know, so Raven was able to continue without having to explain too much.

"So, I was in and out all within one day."

"Shasta has some powerful energy." Bennu noted.

"Oh, you bet." commented Susan. "The image that comes to my mind is those old-fashioned revolving doors. It just whirls you around!"

"And it amps everything up!" Bennu added. "I bet that was quite a combo with your Master Key!"

Scene Thirty-Three: Connections

Susan looked over while chatting with Alex and shot Raven a knowing look.

"OK, wait a minute. What's this Master Key?" Karly asked.

"Well, some months ago I had a session with Susan. Basically, I got a definitive answer on my life purpose. I realized that the culmination of all this healing work, spiritual practice, and ability to intuit symbols was adding up to bringing forward into the world a symbol we have come to know as The Master Key."

"What does this symbol do?" Karly wanted to know.

"It's all about healing, transformation, oneness. It's supposed to help raise the consciousness of humanity somehow. Help people in awakening. Help people really integrate and embody Divine love."

"It's kind of like a powerful tuning fork." Bennu offered. "It holds a vibration that helps make it easier for people to resonate with the emerging consciousness."

"And speaking of tuning forks!" Raven continued, "Oh my gosh! You're not going to believe what happened in San Francisco!"

"What?" Bennu and Karly exclaimed in unison.

"Well, Eve gave me a couple of cryptic intuitive hints. One was about the waterfalls in Shasta, but she also got me to researching *obelisks*. Right before the trip to Shasta I got online and discovered this..." Raven had fired up the iPad2® by now and pulled up the web pages she had visited before. "The Transamerica Building is covered with quartz crystal and has this aluminum pyramid cap at the top. It's this huge super-conductor!"

"What does that mean?" Karly asked.

"It means the building is like a giant hard drive with an intergalactic broadcast station at the top." Bennu was grinning from one ear to the other. "Awesome!"

"I also learned that the Washington Monument has similar construction." Raven added. "The stones magnify and store energy vibrations, and it *also* has an aluminum cap."

"You're not going to go all conspiracy theory on me, are you?" Karly joked.

"No, that's probably somebody else's story." Raven laughed. "Besides there weren't any helicopters chasing us or covert government agencies involved."

"Not that you know of, anyway." Bennu looked half serious.

"So anyway, get this... Susan and I finish our meetings in San Francisco and go over to the Transamerica building just four blocks away. It's pouring down rain. We're getting totally soaked! I go over to this redwood grove and ground the Master Key through the trees into the earth below the tower. Then I go over and put my hand on the building..."

Karly and Bennu were both mersmerized. Susan was enjoying waiting for the punch line. She knew what happened next.

"And I experienced a part of me just *leaving my body*... like my energy just blasted up the side of the building and infused the entire structure with the Master Key energy. I got to the top and just kind of hovered there...then saw myself shooting like a guided missile across the country to the Washington Monument. Once the Master Key reached the next obelisk, it infused itself there, too.

Then I had the weirdest experience..."

"You mean that's not weird enough for you?" Karly chimed in.

Raven and Bennu laughed. Raven continued,

"Well, after the energy kind of soaked in to the Washington Monument and penetrated the earth all around it. I had this vision of seeing myself in the middle of this desert. There was this big ancient obelisk with Egyptian hieroglyphics on it. And what I saw happen to the Transamerica Building also happened to this other one in Egypt. I saw a whole bunch of other obelisks all over the world lighting up and connecting to each other. It was mind blowing..."

Bennu was about to ignite, she was so excited. "Oh my gosh! Oh my gosh! *Oh my gosh!*"

"What's up?" Raven could not imagine what Bennu could be thinking. Bennu's face flushed red like she was having a hot flash. She waved her hands and became short of breath. Bennu took a few deep breaths and got hold of herself.

"You know how I've been doing all this research on Egypt and hieroglyphics for the jewelry I've been working on lately?" her eyes flashed with excitement.

"Yeah. Go on..." Raven encouraged.

Scene Thirty-Three: Connections

"Well, there's this whole story about this ancient city called Heliopolis. It was a real place in Egypt and all the heavy hitters of the time hung out there! You know, like Pythagorus, Plato, Homer... the major philosophers and stuff. Anyway, they believed that every 12,594 years a phoenix would return from the Aisle of Fire and bring a "seed" to place on the Stone of Destiny. Guess where the Stone of Destiny sat?"

Raven and Karly held their collective breath.

"On the top of this huge *obelisk* in Heliopolis!"

Raven felt a huge wave of energy surge over her as all the pieces suddenly flew together like metal shards beneath an industrial strength magnet.

"Oh. My. Gawd..." Raven was stunned. "Do you really think..."

Susan had been keeping one ear to their conversation while talking to Alex.

"Oh yeah, I saw that stone in a museum when I was in Cairo years ago. It's also known as the Ben Ben Stone. It has this really powerful energy." Susan said.

"Ben Ben." Bennu repeated. "You realize that I renamed myself for the bennu bird of Egypt, right? It means, "phoenix.""

"Well, that may explain why we ended up such good friends." Raven smiled.

"Hey, you're the one out there firing up the obelisks!" Bennu laughed. "Looks like the Raven is a Phoenix after all!"

Raven was still marinating in a pool of awe. She tapped on her new iPad2® and searched "Heliopolis_Ben Ben Stone." The image that appeared was exactly what she had seen in her vision in San Francisco.

Karly sat agape, eyes wide. She was swimming in so much mind-blowing information all at once she looked like she might drown trying to grasp it. Was this for real? Was Raven delusional? She was thrilled to be in the inner circle on such an amazing "woo woo" breakthrough. She was also slammed right up against what this meant to her personally.

"So... that's really cool and everything..." Karly paused to determine whether her words were coming off as sincere. "If Raven really *is* the Phoenix... then what happens now? Has anything changed? Are we all gonna get raptured off the planet or are aliens gonna visit or something?"

Raven replied, "That's a good question, Karly. I honestly don't know. I was just following Guidance and doing what my heart led me to do each step of the way. I didn't know anything about this Phoenix business until Bennu just mentioned it. I didn't set out to *be* the Phoenix or fulfill any ancient prophecy. I was just being me and doing my thing, you know?"

Alex had also been listening in on their conversation and thought this would be a good place to join in.

"I remember when I was in grad school in Chicago. This guy came in to demonstrate a prototype of the very first cell phone. He had these two huge wireless "bag phones" in these briefcases, and he said, 'Check this out. I'm going to make a call from this phone and bounce it off a signal tower we have on top of the Sears Tower. And it will ring this other phone.' Everyone sat in amazement as he did just that. The room exploded in applause! It was like being there when Alexander Graham Bell first demonstrated the original telephone. Now, look how far we've come!

Raven, Bennu, and Karly all looked perplexed, wondering where he was going with all this.

"So, here's the connection... Imagine what would have happened back then if a company went out and set up all these cell towers, but almost nobody had cell phones or computers with wireless capability.

"What Raven just did was kind of like that. She brought the whole network online. She made the signal more accessible."

Raven chimed in, "But getting back to Karly's question about 'does this make any difference?', it still all comes down to free will. It's ultimately about *choice*. Okay, so maybe the Master Key has upgraded the signal and now people have better access to a higher level of consciousness... but the choice to access it and apply it is totally up to them."

Alex picked up the theme again. "Just because there's a cel-

Scene Thirty-Three: Connections

lular network in place, doesn't mean you have to go buy a phone, learn how to use it, or make calls on it." I remember when the technology first came out. We had these huge, expensive "brick phones" and not that many people had good coverage. It was hard to reach the people you wanted to reach. People complained about having to 'learn one more darn thing.' I know people today who still keep these very basic phones around 'just for emergencies' while other people run an entire business off their smart phone."

"That's a good point." Bennu jumped in. "People will embrace and integrate this 'soul signal' at whatever level they choose. Some will access it only in emergencies and others will really embody it and use it to live better lives."

"But how will they access it? Nobody even knows it's there!" Karly retorted.

"I have a feeling that may be Raven's next job." Susan hinted with a knowing look to Raven.

"Glad we have another session next week." Raven replied.

"Anyway, Karly, I may not even have to tell people about this for it to be helpful to them. Think of it this way... Let's say one day you have a slow internet connection and then the next day your cable company upgrades you to broadband fiber optic cable. They don't have to tell you about it for you to still enjoy a better connection. You know what I mean? This Master Key signal upgrade will just help people who already have the desire to connect to Divine love and higher consciousness. They can now do so more easily. Maybe that's all there is to it."

"But shouldn't you be out there teaching all about the Master Key and getting people to study it and take seminars and stuff? How are they going to be able to handle all this energy coming in? Isn't it your responsibility to go 'convert' people and help them know what to do with all this?"

Alex jumped in. "Where did you go for training to learn about your cell phone, Karly? Did you need someone to convert you into a cell phone user? Did you need a weekend class to learn how to make a call?"

"Well, no! That's ridiculous! Cell phones are easy. You just push some buttons and call people. They answer or they don't. You 'leave a message at the sound of the beep.'"

"Yeah, and how did you learn how to use it?" Alex pressed.

"I just started messing around with it. I 'butt dialed' a few people from time to time... dropped a few calls. It took awhile to figure out the texting thing with the tiny little keypad, but I got the hang of it."

"So why did you bother to go through all that trouble and take the time to learn it?" Bennu asked.

"Because I wanted to connect to all my friends. When they started doing this stuff and I saw how cool it was to get directions or movie tickets or whatever right off my phone, I wanted in. Sometimes they showed me new things and sometimes I showed them new things. It couldn't be easier." Karly beamed.

"Well, there you go." Raven agreed. "If you make something available to people and they see other people benefitting from it, sometimes they decide to make it their own. It's that simple. No evangelism necessary."

Something was still gnawing at Karly and before she could self-censor she just blurted it out.

"But what makes Raven so special? Why her? I'm thinking I should go see Susan and find out what *my* big special life purpose is! But then again... I don't want to be all full of hubris and grandiosity."

Susan subtly slipped Raven a business card under the table.

"Do you think *I'm* all full of hubris and grandiosity?" Raven replied.

Before Karly could reply, Bennu charged in with a few choice words,

"*Sheesh*, Karly! Raven's been running around in stealth mode her whole freakin' life! Do you have any idea how much Raven has struggled with believing this *really was* her purpose? Do you have any idea how much she's second guessed doing all the things she's done? She's been doing all this stuff quietly behind the scenes and hasn't sought any recognition for any of it. That doesn't sound much like hubris to me! I, for one, am glad she has the courage to come out of hiding, speak her truth, and give her gift to the

Scene Thirty-Three: Connections

world. More of us need to be doing that these days."

Right on cue, Alex offered the technology perspective.

"If you think about it, most of the people who had the biggest impact on our everyday lives never came close to feeling "special." Who knows the names of those who invented the transistor, the silicon chip, or the internet? Can you name any of the people who mapped human DNA? Maybe a few engineers or science geeks could—like me." He said with a hint of sheepishness.

Alex continued, "None of those game changers are household names. None of them had a Messiah complex, you can be sure of that. They didn't set out to 'save the world.' They were just doing what they love to do and wanted to see where it would lead them. Along the way, they discovered some cool stuff that other people could use and build upon. They just played their part, and it was their part to play. Raven's just playing her part."

Bennu added, "And Karly, I think it's awesome you're thinking about discovering your life purpose. Just keep in mind that it will be *unique to you*. Your purpose will look different than Raven's.

Just be warned that once you have that information, you are responsible for what you do with it. It may be so big it overwhelms you. Then again, it may seem so obvious and insignificant you just dismiss it as unimportant. Either way, I can assure you— it will *stretch you!* You will have the opportunity to overcome obstacles and learn many of the lessons you set out to learn in this lifetime. Whether you change the world or not, it will definitely *change you.*

"And that is really the whole point of taking the journey." Raven agreed.

Scene Thirty-Four

Seeds on the Wind

Lying in bed with Isis snuggled at her feet, Raven stared at the ceiling fan above her as she contemplated all of the events and conversations of the past few days. Raven glanced out the window to see the fluffy fairy-like seeds of the neighborhood dandelions floating past.

"Seeds on the wind..." she mused.

She reached for her green leather journal to see if she could make some sense of it all.

"What if..." she wondered, "What if I really *am* the Phoenix and the Master Key really *is* the seed that the prophecy foresaw being placed upon the Stone of Destiny? These myths are entirely symbolic, anyway. Certainly, there was not going to be an actual mythical bird descending from the sky...

"The Phoenix represents transformation and renewal. It represents the Christ Consciousness... the mind and heart of the Divine Child."

Raven realized that every aspect of her life for as long as she could ever remember was a relentless quest for healing, transformation, and becoming an embodiment of Divine Love. Somehow she was integrating, in her own simple and obscure human life, the merging of her relationship with the Divine while fully experiencing daily human life in all its mundane simplicity and unsurpassed beauty. Over the years, she had accomplished exactly what she had seen in her meditation—a gradual falling away of layer after layer of barriers to Love and Light, followed by an opportunity to share that Light with the world.

The more she thought about it, she recognized that so many other people she knew were doing the same thing. The world *was* transforming. Perhaps she had just helped amplify it and accelerate it in some useful way. She was a torchbearer for the Light, one of many — unique perhaps, but not special.

"I wonder if my work is complete... *Was that it?* I spend a lifetime healing and transforming, then intuit a powerful world-transforming symbol, then charge the obelisks of the world to be superconductors for a vibration of wholeness and healing? *Really?*

So, do I just return to my 'regularly scheduled programming' like the television networks do the week after they run all the Christmas specials? It's kind of a let down, really...This must be what astronauts or gold medalists feel like after they accomplish their life's goal. What could I *possibly* do for an encore?"

Raven was amused at the irony that she had just played her part in perhaps one of the most significant events in the history of human consciousness, and almost no one knew! She had found an excellent way to be of service to humanity and the planet and still manage to play "keep away" from the covetous hands of her Ego.

What's more, she would not have to deal with any controversy. She would not have to prove anything or explain any of this improbable weirdness to anyone. She could simply give her gift to the world and consider her life contract fulfilled. With her contribution complete, she could just snuggle up with Alex for the remainder of her days and enjoy the rest of the show!

Raven suspected it might not be that simple. Her biggest clue was the fact that what she had brought forth at this point in time was a "seed."

"Seeds are just the beginning." She mused.

Perhaps that was why she had already scheduled another meeting with Susan Rueppel for this afternoon.

Scene Thirty-Five

The Path Forward

Raven descended carefully down each stair of her apartment building and onto the sidewalk below. Carrying her bike on her shoulder, she did not want to risk a misstep. Her focus was squarely on the ground.

As she prepared to throw her leg over the bicycle, she finally looked upward into the sky. She gasped.

"Oh. My. Gawd."

There, in an otherwise completely empty blue sky, was a huge cloud formation. It was a beautiful and clearly defined *phoenix*.

For several minutes, Raven just stood there with her mouth gaping open in wonder. Then the feeling turned to amusement.

"Very funny. Verrrrrrry funny!" She shook her head as she mounted the bicycle to ride across mid-town. "Susan will get a kick out of this one!"

Raven continued to glance up as she rode — each glance of the giant phoenix cloud made her giggle. She couldn't help but feel she lived a magical life.

Raven locked her bike and entered Susan's office.

"So, are you ready to see what's next?" Susan inquired.

"What could *possibly* be *next?*

You were there in San Francisco. Do you really think there's a second act after *that*?" Raven was incredulous. Before Susan could respond, Raven remembered the cloud.

"Oh! You won't believe this. I stepped outside this morning and there was this huge cloud formation right above me. It filled up most of the sky. Any guess what it was?"

Susan just smiled and waited for it.

"A *phoenix!*"

They both laughed, then Susan answered her question.

"And so you actually think there's no second act after *that*? You're kidding me, right?!"

The two of them sat down at Susan's desk and Susan started her recorder. "So, what's your first question?" Susan asked.

"What's *next*?" Raven replied with a sly smile.

Susan paused for a moment as she accessed the energy of the Master Key.

"Well, it looks like you're going to be writing a book, and you need to get it out before the end of this year."

"A *book*?" Raven looked perplexed. "Are you *kidding*? How could I possibly tell this bizarre story? Who would ever believe it?"

"Haven't you always had all the help you would ever need?" Susan reminded her.

"Well, *yes*." Raven paused and really considered the idea. "Now that I think about it, I could always write it as a 'fictional' story. I could create a few composite characters… compress the time line… no one would ever have to know any of it was actually a real experience. I could get all the important lessons and concepts I've learned woven into this outrageous sounding story that's just a fun ride for the reader. No one would ever have to know!"

"Brilliant!" Susan agreed. "*And no one will ever have to know…*"

Letter from the Author

October 28, 2011

Today marks what many believe to be the official end of the ancient Mayan Calendar (not December 21, 2012). We have been hearing a tremendous amount of rumor and hearsay both in the media at large and among the "illuminutty" for several years now.

By the time this book is officially published on 11-11-11, we will be on the other side of a marker that many perceive energetically as the dawn of a New Golden Age. This is the very beginning of the "post Phoenix" era.

I sat down to write *Return of the Phoenix* the last week of June, 2011. I completed the initial manuscript by September 25, 2011. Start to finish, the writing took exactly 13 weeks. This pace astounded many, including myself, but I had a tremendous sense of urgency to get this story out to the world *now*.

Raven's story was purposely set in the 2010-2011 time frame because I wanted to write and create while immersed in the energy of this historic time. This book not only captures the concerns, technologies, language, and lifestyle decisions of many at this time, it also captures the energetic vibration of this time. Everything feels like it has sped up, and I wanted the pace of the story to reflect that same feeling we have been living through. Most everyone I know feels like they are being catapulted forward and pulled along by unseen forces into the unknown. Some people are scared, others are hopeful, many are just curious, but few agree on what it will all mean.

Personally, I believe a significant shift is taking place in human consciousness. I do not believe, however, it will be a sudden overnight event. I have a feeling the big dates will come and go and we will still be integrating the new software we've been downloading for some time. Nevertheless, we came here now for a reason.

At some level, I believe we all desperately wanted to be here to see what would happen. This is not a spectator sport, this transformation. While I believe we have a lot of energetic support from external forces (Divine, cosmic, and Mother Earth), ultimately I believe that free will reigns and evolution is an inside job. Each of us must decide what we will do with the life we chose to live on the planet at this time.

The Phoenix has returned, the network is online, the signal is strong. Only *you* can choose to connect, participate, and contribute.
I am encouraged by the number of people who, when I tell them the title of this book, exclaim "*I'm* the Phoenix!" Something deep within them recognizes their own power and potential for renewal and transformation and they see themselves in the spirit of this great myth. Collectively, we each represent part of the consciousness the Phoenix represents. Our time has come.

My hope for the reader is that Raven's story will encourage you with a positive vision for these times, and that you will seek to discover and passionately embrace your part in this enormous and wonderful symphony.

All One Love,

Tania

Tania von Allmen

Acknowledgements

One thing most readers will notice about Raven's journey with the Master Key is the number and variety of people who help her along the way. The same has been true for me, and you may notice that Raven and Tania have many of the same friends. Here are some of the very real people who have enriched my journey. **Special thanks to:**

My Family - Husband Alex von Allmen and son Max. Not only have you endured every tumultuous year of my own personal transformation but you have patiently and enthusiastically supported me while writing and editing. I am blessed to share my life with two of the most loving, encouraging, delightful human beings on the planet. Thanks also to Alex for writing the poem in Scene 27.

Ania Brandysiewicz - My mentor and dear friend who taught me how to meditate, how to hear the still small voice of Guidance within, and facilitated much of my own internal healing process. You helped me experience Divine love in order to embody it and live it in the world. I am greatly indebted to you as a teacher and healer.

Susan Rueppel - A colleague and friend who brilliantly and consistently reveals me to myself. You have played such a vital role in helping me bring forth the Master Key with grace and ease. I greatly appreciate your gifts that have helped me expand my vision and step confidently onto my path.

Sheryl McKeown - Truly my "diving buddy" who has been there every step of the way as we explored the sometimes dark and always amusing depths of our being. I have tremendous admiration for your courage, tenacity, and loving heart.

Lisa Kewish - Designer of the amazing moldavite pendant and inspiration for Bennu, you inspire me to step into my creative power and never cease bringing beauty and whimsy into the world.

Yvonne Yoneda Donaldson and the **Sacramento Grandmothers** group - You create sanctuary and hold a space of light and love in an often chaotic world. I greatly appreciate your support, encouragement, and insights.

Members of Healing Artists Network - Susan Rueppel, Laura Hansen, Michael Spackman, Andy Grice, Shannon Cary, Teresa Flint, and Christina Margo. You are all such a tremendous source of insight, healing, and encouragement. I am grateful for your assistance as "ground control" to keep me on track and inspired.

Charles Euchner - Author of *The Writing Code* and my personal writing coach, you showed up at exactly the right moment to get this project off to the best possible start. Your insights and feedback have made this book not only easier to read but much more fun to write.

Thanks to the people who read and provided feedback to the preliminary drafts. Your comments helped shape the final result in helpful and illuminating ways: Lisa Kewish, Ania Brandysiewicz, Susan Rueppel, Karen Parsegian, Yarrow Summer, Susan Bray, Pauline Haynes, MeShell Lane, and Kristin Aplin.

Finally, a word of sincere gratitude to all the benevolent beings on the non-physical plane who work tirelessly (because they don't have to sleep) to facilitate extraordinary support for the rising consciousness of us all. I always received all the help I could ever need, and much of it has come in surprising and delightful ways.

THE MASTER KEY™

The Master Key™ is, in fact, a genuine sacred symbol intuited by author Tania von Allmen. It holds the energy of the emerging consciousness and its core essence is love, healing, and oneness. The author has been working with this symbol in meditation since September of 2010 and is now sharing it with the world.

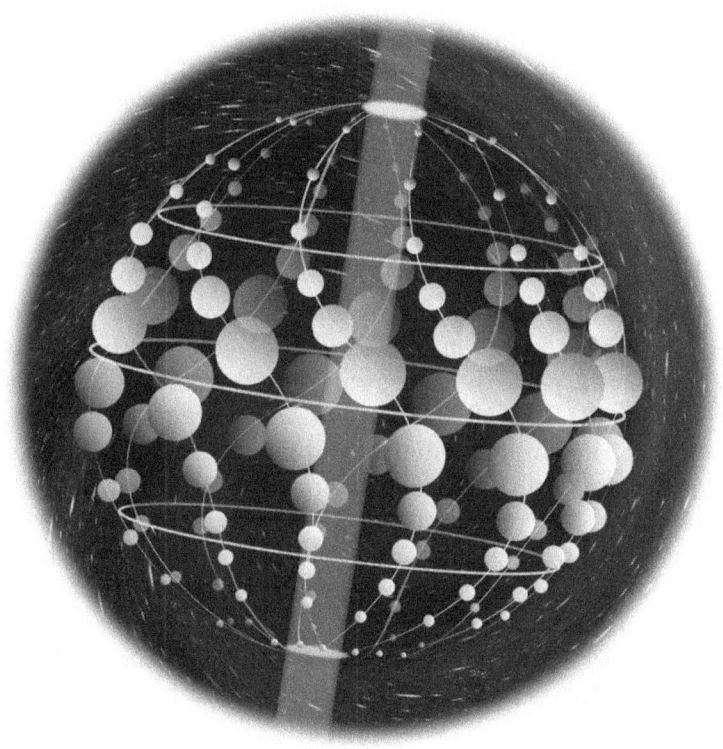

www.MasterKeyJourney.com

Specifications:

The Master Key sacred symbol is comprised of 12 "Rays" (or SubKeys) that each have 12 "Nodes." Each Node has a positive and negative (or masculine and feminine) charge. There are a total of 144 Nodes in the entire structure. Each Ray is a fractal, that is, its structure repeats throughout the whole.

The top hemisphere represents "Above" while the bottom hemisphere represents "Below." The Nodes follow a progression of the Fibonacci sequence (or Divine Proportion) of 1,2,3,5,8,and 13 and progress through the spectrum from red, orange, yellow, green, blue, to violet. (The sequence of the color spectrum reverses between the top hemisphere and the bottom hemisphere.) The spaces between each Node also follow the Fibonacci sequence, only in reverse. So, the distance between the 13 and the 8 is 1, and the distance between the 1 and 2 is 13. The column of white light through the center core connects the two hemispheres, and everything within the structure is connected to everything else.

Implications:

The Master Key symbol is essentially a map of our "Spiritual DNA." There is *so much more* to be discovered about the Master Key and the author expects that more will be understood as our consciousness expands to take it all in. This book was a vehicle to introduce it to the world at a key moment in the evolution of our consciousness.

The story you just read explains not only how The Master Key came to be, but the transformational potential of working with it. Yes, everything Raven experienced and learned was first lived by the author. A few details and characters were subjected to artistic license to improve story flow and protect privacy. Most likely, there will be additional books coming over the next several years that will explore in greater detail the lessons and implications of what The Master Key represents.

Please visit www.MasterKeyJourney.com to learn more about the symbol and working with it yourself. ***Do not reproduce the symbol for commercial use.*** While The Master Key is a gift to the world and you are encouraged to share it with others, it is a violation of copyright and trademark to reproduce it for your own monetary gain. If you are reading a book of this nature, certainly you will do the right thing.

Resources

Much of Raven's story provides a small appetizer for a much meatier banquet of study, practice, and understanding. Here are some resources I have found helpful and reference throughout the story. I encourage you to meet some of her real life friends and also peruse Raven's bookshelf. You can also find direct links to all of these resources at www.MasterKeyJourney.com

Books and audio:
Consciousness and the Evolving Body by Ania Brandysiewicz
San Francisco, Coda, ©2010

Original Prayer: Teachings and Meditations on the Aramaic Words of Jesus audio series, Neal Douglas Klotz
Sounds True Audio, © 2005

The Mayan Calendar and the Transformation of Consciousness by Carl Johan Calleman, Ph.D., Rochester, VT, Bear & Co., ©2004

The Order of Melchizedek by Dan Chesbro
Scotland, UK, Findhorn Press, ©2010

What Tom Sawyer Learned from Dying by Sidney Saylor Farr, Norfolk, VA, Hampton Roads Publishing, © 1993

A Call to Power: The Grandmothers Speak by Sharon McErlane
Net of Light Press, ©2006

Hand Me a Wrench, My Life is Out of Whack by Laura Hansen
Elk Grove, CA, Taylor Hill Press, ©2010

The Crystal Bible: A Definitive Guide to Crystals by Judy Hall
Cincinnati, OH, Walking Stick Press, ©2003

The Writing Code by Charles Euchner
available at Amazon.com in Kindle edition, ©2010

Professional Services Cited in *Return of the Phoenix:*

Symbol Design and Soul Print service by Tania von Allmen
www.LuminosityStudio.com

Business and Medical Intuition service by Susan Rueppel
www.ChiefIntuitionOfficer.com

Isedo (scene 8) **session** by Ania Brandysiewicz
www.SchoolOfCreation.com
also Sheryl McKeown at www.AskListenDo.com

Intuitive Jewelry Design (like Bennu) by Lisa Kewish
www.kewishdesigns.blogspot.com

Book Web Sites for *Return of the Phoenix*:
www.ThePhoenixReturns.com
www.MasterKeyJourney.com

The author will be introducing more materials for personal study such as a book club workbook, items for working with the Master Key symbol, and other related resources. Please visit one of these web sites and subscribe to the mailing list to get the latest updates.

Speaking: Would you like to have Tania speak to your group? You can reach her courtesy of Sun Runner Publishing at: Phoenix@SunRunnerPublishing.com

Return of the Phoenix: Journey of the Master Key is also available for Kindle at Amazon.com or through SunRunnerPublishing.com

www.ingramcontent.com/pod-product-compliance
Lightning Source LLC
Chambersburg PA
CBHW071705090426
42738CB00009B/1668